180 DAYS® of Reading for Fifth Grade

Authors

Kathy Kopp, M.S.Ed.

Dylan Levsey

Program Credits

Corinne Burton, M.A.Ed., *President and Publisher*
Emily R. Smith, *SVP of Content Development*
Véronique Bos, *Vice President of Creative*
Lynette Ordoñez, *Content Manager*
Ashley Oberhaus, M.Ed., *Content Specialist*
Melissa Laughlin, *Editor*
David Slayton, Assistant Editor
Jill Malcolm, *Graphic Designer*

Image Credits: p.49 Shutterstock/James Kirkikis; p.102 Wikimedia/Andrew Z. Colvin; p.103 ESO/EHT Collaboration; p.120 Shutterstock/Mai Groves; p.121 Shutterstock/Fotos593; p.140 Shutterstock/photoyh; p.157 Shutterstock/Belish; p.175 Shutterstock/Nuamfolio; p.212 Shutterstock/TACHEFOTO; all other images Shutterstock and/or iStock

Printed by: 465482
Printed in : Malaysia
PO#: 25082

Standards

© Copyright 2010 National Governors Association Center for Best Practices and Council of Chief State School Officers. All rights reserved.
© Copyright 2007–2023 Texas Education Agency (TEA). All Rights Reserved.
© 2023 TESOL International Association
© 2023 Board of Regents of the University of Wisconsin System
© 2023 International Society for Technology in Education (ISTE), iste.org. All Rights Reserved.

The classroom teacher may reproduce copies of materials in this book for classroom use only. The reproduction of any part for an entire school or school system is strictly prohibited. No part of this publication may be transmitted, stored, or recorded in any form without written permission from the publisher.

Website addresses included in this book are public domain and may be subject to changes or alterations of content after publication of this product. Shell Education does not take responsibility for the future accuracy or relevance and appropriateness of website addresses included in this book. Please contact the company if you come across any inappropriate or inaccurate website addresses, and they will be corrected in product reprints.

All companies, websites, and products mentioned in this book are registered trademarks of their respective owners or developers and are used in this book strictly for editorial purposes. No commercial claim to their use is made by the author(s) or the publisher.

Shell Education
A division of Teacher Created Materials
5482 Argosy Avenue
Huntington Beach, CA 92649
www.tcmpub.com/shell-education
ISBN 979-8-7659-1807-4
© 2024 Shell Educational Publishing, Inc.

Table of Contents

Introduction

The Need for Practice

To be successful in today's reading classroom, students must deeply understand both concepts and procedures so that they can discuss and demonstrate their understanding. Demonstrating understanding is a process that must be continually practiced for students to be successful. According to Robert Marzano, "Practice has always been, and always will be, a necessary ingredient to learning procedural knowledge at a level at which students execute it independently" (2010, 83). Practice is especially important to help students apply reading comprehension strategies and word-study skills. *180 Days of Reading* offers teachers and parents a full page of reading comprehension and word recognition practice activities for each day of the school year.

The Science of Reading

For some people, reading comes easily. They barely remember how it happened. For others, learning to read takes more effort.

The goal of reading research is to understand the differences in how people learn to read and find the best ways to help all students learn. The term *Science of Reading* is commonly used to refer to this body of research. It helps people understand how to provide instruction in learning the code of the English language, how to develop fluency, and how to navigate challenging text and make sense of it.

Much of this research has been around for decades. In fact, in the late 1990s, Congress commissioned a review of the reading research. In 2000, the National Reading Panel (NRP) published a report that became the backbone of the Science of Reading. The NRP report highlights five components of effective reading instruction. These include the following:

- **Phonemic Awareness:** understanding and manipulating individual speech sounds
- **Phonics:** matching sounds to letters for use in reading and spelling
- **Fluency:** reading connected text accurately and smoothly
- **Vocabulary:** knowing the meanings of words in speech and in print
- **Reading Comprehension:** understanding what is read

There are two commonly referenced frameworks that build on reading research and provide a visual way for people to understand what is needed to learn to read. In the mid-1980s, a framework called the Simple View of Reading was introduced (Gough and Tunmer 1986). It shows that reading comprehension is possible when students are able to decode (or read) the words and have the language to understand the words.

The Simple View of Reading

Decoding × Language Comprehension = Reading Comprehension

Another framework that builds on the research behind the Science of Reading is Scarborough's Reading Rope (Scarborough 2001). It shows specific skills needed for both language comprehension and word recognition. The "strands" of the rope for language comprehension include having background content knowledge, knowing vocabulary, understanding language structure, having verbal reasoning, and understanding literacy. Word recognition includes phonological awareness, decoding skills, and sight recognition of familiar words (Scarborough 2001). As individual skills are strengthened and practiced, they become increasingly strategic and automatic to promote reading comprehension.

© Shell Education

The Science of Reading *(cont.)*

Many parts of our understanding of how people learn to read stand the test of time and have been confirmed by more recent studies. However, new research continues to add to the understanding of reading. Some of this research shows the importance of wide reading (reading about a variety of topics), motivation, and self-regulation. The conversation will never be over, as new research will continue to refine the understanding of how people learn to read. There is always more to learn!

180 Days of Reading has been informed by this reading research. This series provides opportunities for students to practice the skills that years of research indicate contribute to reading growth. There are several features in this book that are supported by the Science of Reading.

Text Selection

- Carefully chosen texts offer experiences in a **wide range of text types**. Each unit includes nonfiction, fiction, and a nontraditional text type or genre (e.g., letters, newspaper articles, advertisements, menus).
- Texts intentionally build upon one another to help students **build background knowledge** from day to day.
- Engaging with texts on the same topic for a thematic unit enables students to become familiar with related **vocabulary**, **language structure**, and **literacy knowledge**. This allows reading to become increasingly strategic and automatic, leading to better **fluency** and **comprehension**.

Activity Design

- Specific **language comprehension** and **word-recognition skills** are reinforced throughout the activities.
- Each text includes a purpose for reading and an opportunity to practice various reading strategies through annotation. This promotes **close reading** of the text.
- Paired fiction and nonfiction texts are used to promote **comparison** and encourage students to **make connections** between texts within a unit.
- Students **write to demonstrate understanding** of the texts. Students provide written responses in a variety of forms, including short answers, open-ended responses, and creating their own versions of nontraditional texts.

This book provides the regular practice of reading skills that students need as they develop into excellent readers.

How to Use This Resource

Unit Structure Overview

This resource is organized into twelve units. Each three-week unit follows a consistent format for ease of use.

Week 1: Nonfiction

Day 1	Students read nonfiction and answer multiple-choice questions.
Day 2	Students read nonfiction and answer multiple-choice questions.
Day 3	Students read nonfiction and answer multiple-choice, short-answer, and open-response questions.
Day 4	Students read a longer nonfictional text, answer multiple-choice questions, and complete graphic organizers.
Day 5	Students reread the text from Day 4 and answer reading-response questions.

Week 2: Fiction

Day 1	Students read fiction and answer multiple-choice questions.
Day 2	Students read fiction and answer multiple-choice questions.
Day 3	Students read fiction and answer multiple-choice, short-answer, and open-response questions.
Day 4	Students read a longer fictional text, answer multiple-choice questions, and complete graphic organizers.
Day 5	Students reread the text from Day 4 and answer reading-response questions.

Week 3: Nontraditional Text

Day 1	Students read nontraditional text and answer multiple-choice and open-response questions.
Day 2	Students complete close-reading activities with paired texts from the unit.
Day 3	Students complete close-reading activities with paired texts from the unit.
Day 4	Students create their own nontraditional texts.
Day 5	Students write their own versions of the nontraditional text from Day 1.

 © Shell Education

How to Use This Resource *(cont.)*

Unit Structure Overview *(cont.)*

Paired Texts

State standards have brought into focus the importance of preparing students for college and career success by expanding their critical-thinking and analytical skills. It is no longer enough for students to read and comprehend a single text on a topic. Rather, the integration of ideas across texts is crucial for a more comprehensive understanding of themes presented by authors.

Literacy specialist Jennifer Soalt has written that paired texts are "uniquely suited to scaffolding and extending students' comprehension" (2005, 680). She identifies three ways in which paired fiction and nonfiction are particularly effective in increasing comprehension: the building of background knowledge, the development of vocabulary, and the increase in student motivation (Soalt 2005).

Each three-week unit in *180 Days of Reading* is connected by a common theme or topic. Packets of each week's or each unit's practice pages can be prepared for students.

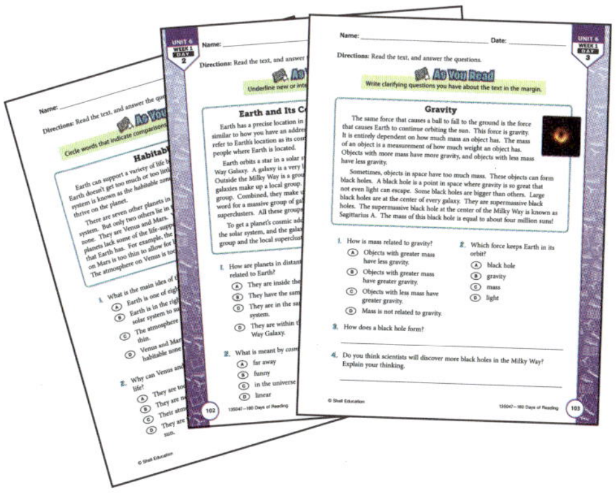

During Week 1, students read nonfictional texts and answer questions.

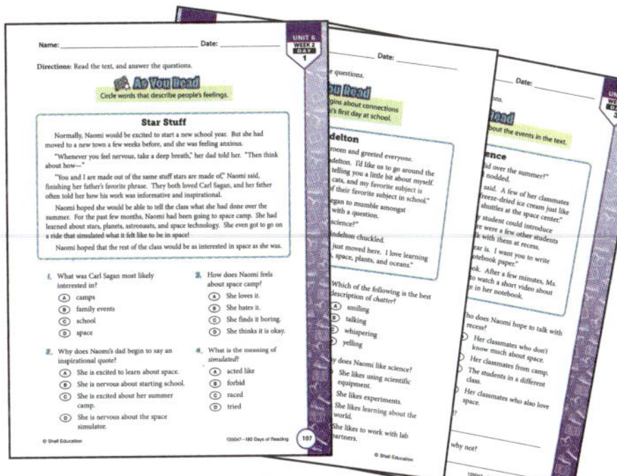

During Week 2, students read fictional texts and answer questions.

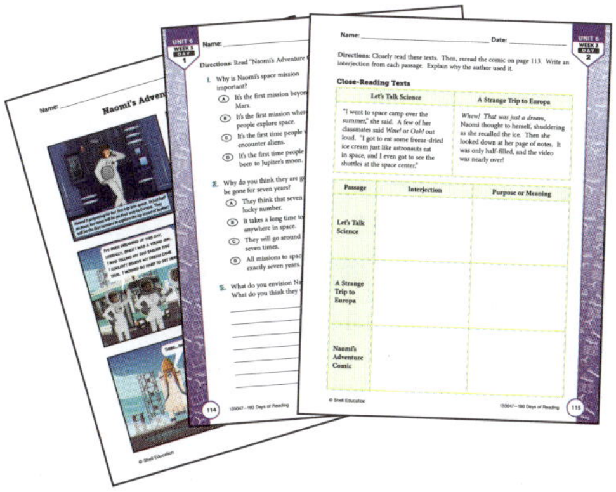

During Week 3, students read nontraditional texts (advertisements, poems, letters, etc.), answer questions, and complete close-reading and writing activities.

How to Use This Resource *(cont.)*

Student Practice Pages

Practice pages reinforce grade-level skills across a variety of reading concepts for each day of the school year. Each day's reading activity is provided as a full practice page, making them easy to prepare and implement as part of a morning routine, at the beginning of each reading lesson, or as homework.

Practice Pages for Weeks 1 and 2

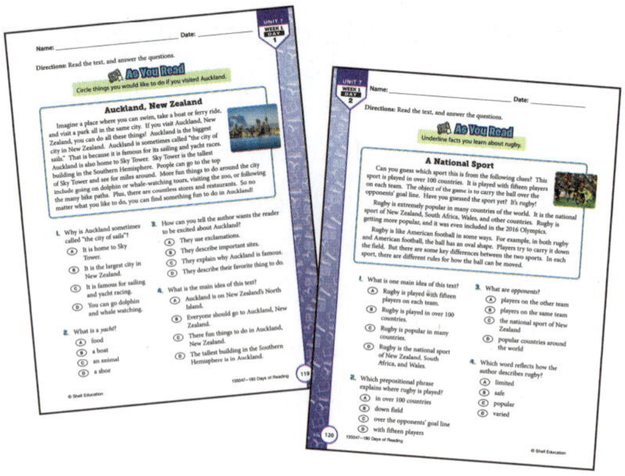

Days 1 and 2 of each week follow a consistent format, with a short text passage and multiple-choice questions.

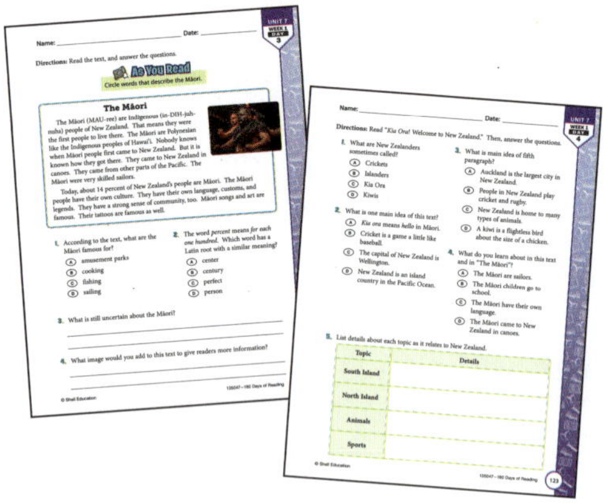

Days 3 and 4 have a combination of multiple-choice, short-answer, and open-response questions.

On day 5, students complete text-based writing prompts.

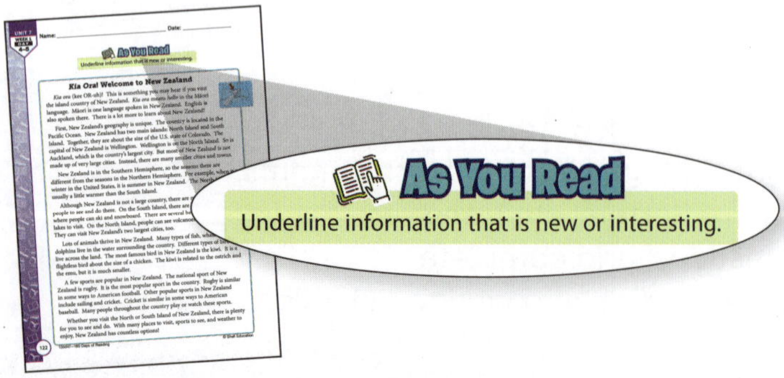

The As You Read activities give students a purpose for reading the texts and provide opportunities to practice various reading skills and strategies.

© Shell Education

How to Use This Resource *(cont.)*

Student Practice Pages *(cont.)*

Practice Pages for Week 3

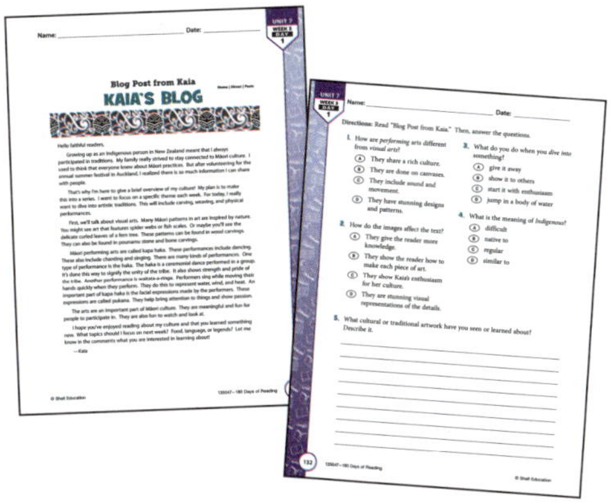

Day 1 of this week follows a consistent format, with a nontraditional text and multiple-choice and open-response questions.

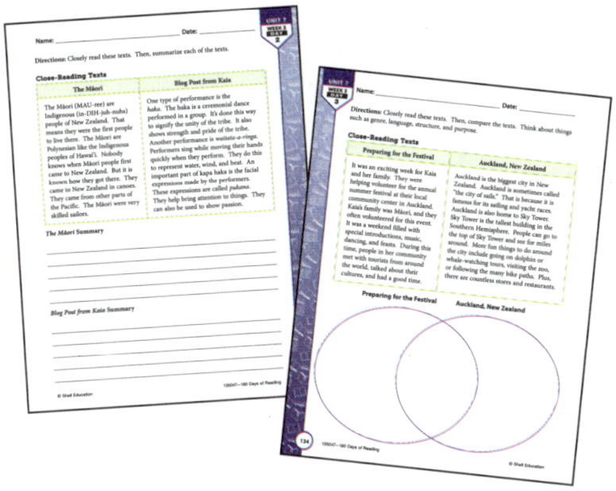

On days 2 and 3, students engage in close-reading activities of paired texts. Students are encouraged to compare and contrast different aspects of the texts they read throughout the unit.

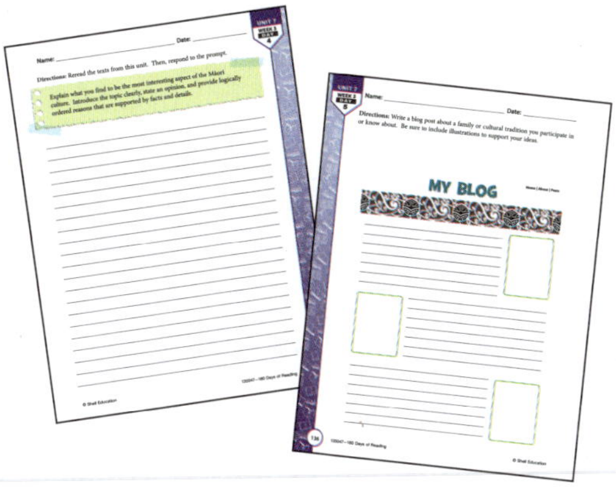

On days 4 and 5, students think about the texts in the unit, respond to a writing prompt, and construct their own versions of diverse texts. Students are encouraged to use information from texts throughout the unit to inspire and support their writing.

Instructional Options

180 Days of Reading is a flexible resource that can be used in various instructional settings for different purposes.

- Use these student pages as daily warm-up activities or as review.
- Work with students in small groups, allowing them to focus on specific skills. This setting also lends itself to partner and group discussions about the texts.
- Student pages in this resource can be completed independently during center times and as activities for early finishers.

How to Use This Resource *(cont.)*

Diagnostic Assessment

The practice pages in this book can be used as diagnostic assessments. These activity pages require students to think critically, respond to text-dependent questions, and utilize reading and writing skills and strategies. (An answer key for the practice pages is provided starting on page 230.)

For each unit, analysis sheets are provided as *Microsoft Word®* files in the digital resources. There is a *Class Analysis Sheet* and an *Individual Analysis Sheet*. Use the file that matches your assessment needs. After each week, record how many answers each student got correct on the unit's analysis sheet. Only record the answers for the multiple-choice questions. The written-response questions and graphic organizers can be evaluated using the writing rubric or other evaluation tools (see below). At the end of each unit, analyze the data on the analysis sheet to determine instructional focuses for your child or class.

The diagnostic analysis tools included in the digital resources allow for quick evaluation and ongoing monitoring of student work. See at a glance which reading genre students may need to focus on further to develop proficiency.

Using the Results to Differentiate Instruction

Once results are gathered and analyzed, use the data to inform the way to differentiate instruction. The data can help determine which concepts are the most difficult for students and that need additional instructional support and continued practice.

The results of the diagnostic analysis may show that an entire class is struggling with a particular genre. If these concepts have been taught in the past, this indicates that further instruction or reteaching is necessary. If these concepts have not been taught yet, this data is a great preassessment and demonstrates that students do not have a working knowledge of the concepts.

The results of the diagnostic analysis may also show that an individual or small group of students is struggling with a particular concept or group of concepts. Consider pulling aside these students while others are working independently to instruct further on the concept(s). You can also use the results to help identify individuals or groups of proficient students who are ready for enrichment or above-grade-level instruction. These students may benefit from independent learning contracts or more challenging activities.

Writing Rubric

A rubric for written responses is provided on page 229. Display the rubric for students to reference as they write. Score students' written responses, and provide them with feedback on their writing.

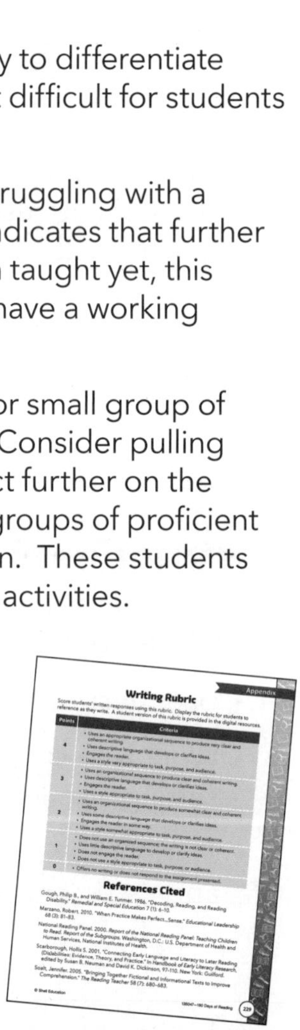
Appendix

Writing Rubric

References Cited

© Shell Education

Name: ______________________ Date: ______________

Directions: Read the text, and answer the questions.

As You Read

Identify a cause-effect relationship. Circle the cause. Underline the effect.

What Do You Eat for Breakfast?

Eating breakfast is an important part of staying healthy and active. This is because people's bodies require energy to function. People get energy by eating food. Bodies use that energy to help people grow, move, and think. When someone eats a healthy breakfast, their brain works better. They can learn more and do better in school. Eating a healthy breakfast can also help people avoid feeling hungry a couple hours later. Plus, eating a healthy breakfast gives a person more energy. Certain food choices will give a person more energy than others. This way, they can enjoy doing more things.

Even though it may be easy to skip breakfast, don't do it! Breakfast is an important meal. It has many benefits.

1. Which type of image would tell a reader more about this text?
   - (A) a picture of a hand
   - (B) a picture of a healthy breakfast
   - (C) a fast-food menu
   - (D) a daily schedule

2. Which prepositional phrase best completes this sentence?

   A healthy breakfast is an important part ______ everyone's day.
   - (A) by
   - (B) for
   - (C) from
   - (D) of

3. Why is eating breakfast important?
   - (A) Your body gets the energy it needs if you eat breakfast.
   - (B) Your brain does not work well if you eat breakfast.
   - (C) You get very hungry if you eat breakfast.
   - (D) It is hard to make good food choices if you eat breakfast.

4. What does it mean to avoid something?
   - (A) buy it
   - (B) you may like it
   - (C) try to make it
   - (D) stay away from it

Name: ______________________________ Date: ________________

Directions: Read the text, and answer the questions.

As You Read

Underline three important points the author makes.

Healthy Breakfast Choices

There are many healthy choices for foods to eat at breakfast. One good choice is eggs. Eggs have a lot of protein, and protein helps bodies grow. Protein is also important for making muscles strong. Protein helps to stop hunger, so a person can feel more satisfied when they eat a meal with protein. Some people prefer to eat fresh fruit for breakfast. This can be a good choice as well, but fruit does not have as much protein as eggs. Including fruit is a good way to balance your breakfast. For example, a banana can be paired with high-protein yogurt.

It is best to avoid eating only high-fat foods for breakfast, such as doughnuts or cinnamon rolls. Of course, it is fine to have one of these treats occasionally. However, these sweet treats do not satisfy hunger for very long. Pairing them with a protein can help. But they are not recommended to eat every day.

In everyday life, it is wise to choose a breakfast that has whole grains, fruit, and protein. What will you have for breakfast tomorrow?

1. How are eggs and fresh fruit different?
   - (A) Eggs have more protein.
   - (B) Eggs are high in fat.
   - (C) Fresh fruit has protein.
   - (D) Fresh fruit is high in fat.

2. Why is it best to avoid high-fat breakfast foods?
   - (A) They have a lot of protein.
   - (B) They include whole grains.
   - (C) They are too expensive.
   - (D) They do not satisfy hunger.

3. Which means the opposite of *wise*?
   - (A) better
   - (B) foolish
   - (C) smaller
   - (D) smarter

4. What does it mean if something satisfies your hunger?
   - (A) It tastes delicious.
   - (B) It stops your hunger.
   - (C) It takes a long time to eat.
   - (D) It makes you feel hungrier.

 © Shell Education

Name: ______________________ Date: ______________

Directions: Read the text, and answer the questions.

As You Read

Place a plus sign (+) by important information about cereal.

Cereal: A Popular Food Choice

One very popular food choice for breakfast is cereal. Cereal is convenient because it is effortless to make, and it does not take long to eat. Some kinds of cereal are very good for you. For example, cereals made with whole grains help keep people's hearts healthy. Whole grains give people's bodies energy. Some cereals have dried fruit and nuts in them, and those are also good choices.

Choosing a cereal carefully is important. Some cereals have lots of sugar, but they do not have many whole grains. Those cereals are not good for you. It is best to choose a cereal that does not have a lot of sugar. Eating too much sugar can be bad for a person's health, and sugar does not provide long-lasting energy.

There are so many options to choose from in stores. You may end up having a hard time deciding which one to choose because they all look tasty!

1. How can cereals with whole grains help your body?
   - (A) They help you to see better.
   - (B) They help you to hear better.
   - (C) They help your bones grow.
   - (D) They help keep your heart healthy.

2. How does the word *effortless* apply to the text?
   - (A) Cereal is healthy.
   - (B) Cereal tastes good.
   - (C) Cereal is easy to make.
   - (D) Cereal has fruits and nuts.

3. How can cereal be part of a healthy breakfast? ______________________________

____

4. Would the author find your favorite cereal to be healthy or not very healthy? Use evidence from the text to explain why.

____

____

Name: ______________________ Date: ______________

As You Read

Circle the problem that Kellogg solved. Underline the solution to the problem.

The Cereal Man

Did you have cereal for breakfast this morning? If you did, you're not alone. Millions of people eat cereal for breakfast every day. In fact, cereal is popular all over the world. It all started with one man, William Keith Kellogg.

Kellogg was born on April 7, 1860, in Battle Creek, Michigan. His first job was stocking shelves at the Battle Creek Sanitarium. A sanitarium is similar to a hospital. People who have been ill for a long time or people who are getting over a serious illness stay there. When Kellogg grew up, he became the manager of the sanitarium. His brother, John, was the chief doctor there.

One big problem at the sanitarium was the patients' diets. The patients needed healthy diets, but it was also important for their food to taste good. Kellogg tried to find a good food choice to take the place of bread. But he was having a hard time finding a replacement.

By accident, Kellogg found something even better than bread. He left some wheat cooking too long. When it was rolled out, it formed large, thin flakes. He decided to give it a try. He asked his brother to serve it to the patients, and they loved it! In fact, they liked it so much that they wanted breakfast flakes sent to them even after they left the sanitarium. So, Kellogg started a new business in 1884. He sold packaged breakfast flakes. And before long, Kellogg's breakfast cereal was popular in other countries, too.

Kellogg did more than just create breakfast flakes. His company made a lot of money. Kellogg used most of it to help children. He also used his money to help several other charities.

Kellogg died in 1951. But his most famous invention is as popular as ever. Kellogg would probably be surprised to see how many kinds of breakfast cereals there are today!

 © Shell Education

Name: ______________________ Date: ____________

Directions: Read "The Cereal Man." Then, answer the questions.

1. What did Kellogg do before he became manager of the sanitarium?
   - (A) He stocked shelves.
   - (B) He started a new company.
   - (C) He invented breakfast flakes.
   - (D) He used his money to help children.

2. How did Kellogg "hit the nail on the head" with his invention?
   - (A) He was able to quit his job at the sanitarium.
   - (B) He was able to make more bread at the sanitarium.
   - (C) He solved a problem for people in the sanitarium.
   - (D) He could go back to stocking shelves at the sanitarium.

3. Why was it so important for the patients' food to taste good?
   - (A) People needed to eat more food.
   - (B) People could not find healthy food.
   - (C) People did not want to eat food that was healthy.
   - (D) People would not eat healthy food that didn't taste good.

4. Why might the author describe Kellogg as *generous*?
   - (A) He gave money to help people.
   - (B) He made a lot of money making cereal.
   - (C) He invented something that others needed.
   - (D) He discovered breakfast flakes by mistake.

5. Write four major events in Kellogg's life. Write them in the order they occurred.

Event 1	Kellogg was born on April 7, 1860, in Battle Creek, Michigan.
Event 2	
Event 3	
Event 4	

Name: ______________________ Date: ____________

Directions: Reread "The Cereal Man" and the earlier texts from this week. Then, respond to the prompt.

Write to explain what you think is the best breakfast option that anyone can make. Use details and evidence from one or more texts to support your ideas.

© Shell Education

Name: ______________________ Date: ____________

Directions: Read the text, and answer the questions.

As You Read

Write and circle words that describe Henry based on his thoughts and actions.

The Cereal Box Competition

Henry usually read the back of the cereal box as he ate breakfast in the mornings. He enjoyed the fun puzzles and word searches. But he had never felt so drawn to the text on the back until this morning.

The box read: *Create a custom cereal box, and enter for your chance to win a video game console.* Henry had never entered a competition like this before. Nothing had motivated him to enter one before. However, Henry really wanted a new gaming console, and his dad always said they were too hard to find. So, maybe he would give this competition a shot. He was pretty sure he wouldn't win, but he wanted to try anyway.

After school, Henry drew up some quick ideas for a cereal box. Then, he filled out his information on the back of the box, cut it out, and put it in an envelope. He wrote his address, included a stamp, and placed the envelope in the mailbox. Now, all he had to do was wait.

1. Why does Henry never enter a competition?

- (A) His dad discourages it.
- (B) He is not creative enough.
- (C) He never has a reason to.
- (D) He is certain he would not win.

2. How does Henry feel about the chance of winning a video game console?

- (A) confident
- (B) doubtful
- (C) enthusiastic
- (D) humbled

3. What is something that may be *custom-made*?

- (A) jewelry
- (B) pet dog
- (C) movie
- (D) stapler

4. What is an antonym for *motivate*?

- (A) create
- (B) discourage
- (C) inspire
- (D) try

Name: ______________________ Date: ______________

Directions: Read the text, and answer the questions.

As You Read

Underline a problem or conflict in the story. Circle the solution.

Henry's Luck

Four months had passed since Henry mailed in his envelope. A lot had happened since then! He was in the second half of his fifth-grade year, he got a new dog, and his dad had started a new job.

He didn't tell anyone about it, but he got into a weird habit of wearing his lucky socks as often as he could. They had four-leaf clovers on them, and he hoped they would bring him luck in winning the competition.

One of Henry's chores was to check the mail every day. He never received anything for himself—until today. When he grabbed the mail after dinner, he saw his name on one of the envelopes. He looked at the return address, and his eyes went wide when he realized it was for the cereal box competition.

1. How might Henry feel about the mail he receives?
   - (A) annoyed
   - (B) heartbroken
   - (C) hopeful
   - (D) miserable

2. What makes Henry's habit strange?
   - (A) Henry's friends never wear the same socks twice.
   - (B) Most people do not wear the same socks every day.
   - (C) Henry's dog is fond of chewing on his socks.
   - (D) Henry's dad wears his lucky socks to his new job, too.

3. How does Henry feel about winning the competition?
   - (A) He is cautiously optimistic.
   - (B) He doesn't feel confident.
   - (C) He doesn't think he should have entered.
   - (D) He knows he will win without a doubt.

4. Which word best describes Henry's habit?
   - (A) customary
   - (B) forgiving
   - (C) normal
   - (D) superstitious

© Shell Education

Name: ____________________ Date: ______________

Directions: Read the text, and answer the questions.

As You Read

Circle a cause. Underline its effect.

Siblings

Henry was too nervous to open the envelope and read the letter himself.

"Why, are you afraid of it?" his sister asked.

"I'm just too nervous!" Henry exclaimed, waving the envelope. She sighed and held out her palm, so Henry gave it to her with shaking hands.

He felt like time had stopped as he watched her tear into the envelope. He watched her face for signs of excitement, but she didn't show any. In fact, she actually looked disappointed! She frowned and shook her head slowly.

Henry's face fell, and he took the letter from her so he could confirm the devastating loss for himself. *Dear Henry*, the letter began, *Congratulations for winning the cereal box competition!*

"I don't believe it!" Henry yelled in excitement.

His sister smirked and gave Henry a fist bump. Not only had he won the gaming console, but the letter stated he had also won a tour of the local cereal factory, a year's worth of cereal, and a chance to create his *own* cereal!

1. How does Henry's sister trick him?
   - (A) She tells him he did not win.
   - (B) She hides the letter.
   - (C) She says the letter is blank.
   - (D) She fakes disappointment.

2. What is an antonym for *frowned*?
   - (A) grinned
   - (B) opened
   - (C) scowled
   - (D) wrinkled

3. What surprises Henry? ______________________________

____

4. What would you hope to win in a competition? Why?

____

____

Name: ______________________________ Date: ________________

As You Read

Circle words that indicate time-order events.

Henry's Gummy Flakes

The day of the tour had arrived! An employee named Samantha greeted them. She took them to a room upstairs with a custom cereal selection screen.

Henry pressed the button to select his base ingredients. First, he began reading over all the possible main ingredients: cornflakes, rice, and wheat squares. He selected cornflakes. The next screen that popped up allowed him to choose from the following additional ingredients: pecans, walnuts, assorted berries, strawberries, raisins, dried bananas, marshmallows, chocolate chips, and gummy worms! Henry had so many ideas. But first, he chose marshmallows. Then, he decided to add chocolate chips and gummy worms. Finally, he selected walnuts and assorted berries.

Henry watched his custom cereal being made. There were three machines connected to a conveyor belt. The largest machine had a series of three tubes connected to the back of it. At the front, a single tube came out of the machine.

Henry asked, "Is that where the main ingredients are added?"

"That's correct!" Samantha replied. "Each of the three tubes connects to one of the main ingredients. To start, each tube brings a separate main ingredient forward. Some people like to mix the main ingredients. This machine can mix them together. Then, the cereal slides down the tube in the front and into a container. The conveyor belt moves it to the next machine in line."

Then, Samantha pointed to the center machine. "This is where the additional ingredients are added and mixed in."

Samantha pointed to the last machine. She said, "The smallest one is used to give the cereal a final mixing. Finally, it goes into the custom-made cereal box you sent in for the competition."

Henry and his parents watched as the cereal was mixed and transported into the smaller machine. After a few moments, the bottom of the machine opened up. They went to retrieve a box of Henry's custom-made cereal.

At home, Henry poured everyone a bowl of cereal. Henry loved every bite he took. It seemed like Henry's parents enjoyed it, too—as long as they ate around the gummy worms.

 © Shell Education

Name: ______________________ Date: ______________

Directions: Read "Henry's Gummy Flakes." Then, answer the questions.

1. How does Henry feel as his custom cereal is being made?
   - Ⓐ concerned
   - Ⓑ excited
   - Ⓒ grateful
   - Ⓓ perplexed

2. What do Henry's parents think of his cereal?
   - Ⓐ They like everything but the gummy worms.
   - Ⓑ They are surprised the berries taste good.
   - Ⓒ They do not like the cereal very much.
   - Ⓓ They wish he had used rice as the base ingredient.

3. Which word uses the prefix the same way as in the word *transport*?
   - Ⓐ entranced
   - Ⓑ export
   - Ⓒ strands
   - Ⓓ transmit

4. What does a conveyor belt do?
   - Ⓐ empties objects from one bin to another
   - Ⓑ heats objects to prepare them for baking
   - Ⓒ cools objects to prepare them for mixing
   - Ⓓ transports objects from one place to another

5. Write events that occur at the cereal factory in the order they happened.

Challenge or Task	Henry has to design his own cereal.
Event	
Event	
Event	
Resolution	

© Shell Education

Name: ______________________________ Date: ________________

Directions: Reread "Henry's Gummy Flakes." Then, respond to the prompt.

Write a story about a time when you made something for breakfast or another meal. Use a variety of transitional words, phrases, and clauses to write about the sequence of events.

© Shell Education

Name: ______________________ Date: ______________

Back of the Cereal Box

HENRY'S GUMMY FLAKES

*designed as part of a contest prize

Meet the Cereal Creator

Name: Henry

Age: 11

Favorite Cereal: Any with marshmallows!

Fun Fact: My dad went on a cereal factory tour when he was a kid, too!

When I was given the opportunity to create my own cereal, I knew that I wanted to make a fun treat that my friends and I would love. But I also wanted one that had never been done before. That's why my cereal is made of cornflakes. I also mixed in some chocolate chips, marshmallows, and gummy worms. I hope you love this cereal as much as I do!

- Henry

Words

Henry
grain
sugar
chocolate
marshmallow
prize
tour
cereal

R R O P D U O Z I T U W
F Z C N T R B B O D G O
F Q L D Q R A U L Q K L
D V Q K X V R G H Y V L
R T Y K C L P L U U G A
U N I A R G A R N S G M
Y A T U M E G M I R X H
H P D H R T L M H Z E S
E P M E I W Z K Y V E R
N W C H O C O L A T E A
R Q M E U A F I E D D M
Y B Z P J P H F I E O I

Name: ____________________ Date: ____________

Directions: Read "Back of the Cereal Box." Then, answer the questions.

1. What inspires Henry's cereal?
   - (A) He wants it to be fun and unique.
   - (B) He wants it to be chewy and crunchy.
   - (C) He wants it to be sweet and sour.
   - (D) He wants it to have fruit and rice.

2. How is Henry's point of view shown in the note?
   - (A) He is excited for others to try his cereal.
   - (B) He wants to motivate others to make their own cereal.
   - (C) He hopes to inspire cereal makers to make his cereal.
   - (D) He tries to convince readers that his cereal is the best.

3. Which of the following is an example of an opportunity?
   - (A) sleeping
   - (B) visiting close relatives
   - (C) attending a cool science camp
   - (D) going to the dentist

4. Which ingredient is most likely Henry's favorite?
   - (A) almonds
   - (B) marshmallows
   - (C) rice
   - (D) berries

5. Would you like to try Henry's cereal? Explain why or why not.

____

____

____

____

____

____

____

____

____

© Shell Education

Name: ______________________________ Date: ______________

Directions: Closely read these texts. Draw additional items to build a more complete breakfast for Henry. Label the items and explain why you included them.

Close-Reading Texts

Healthy Breakfast Choices	Back of the Cereal Box
There are many healthy choices for foods to eat at breakfast. One good choice is eggs. Eggs have a lot of protein, and protein helps bodies grow. Protein is also important for making muscles strong. Protein helps to stop hunger, so a person can feel more satisfied when they eat a meal with protein. Some people prefer to eat fresh fruit for breakfast. This can be a good choice as well, but fruit does not have as much protein as eggs. Including fruit is a good way to balance your breakfast.	When I created my own cereal, I knew that I wanted to make a fun treat that my friends and I would love. But I also wanted to make a cereal that had never been created before, of course. That's why I started my cereal with cornflakes, but then I got creative. I also mixed in some chocolate chips, marshmallows, and gummy worms. I hope you love this cereal as much as I do!

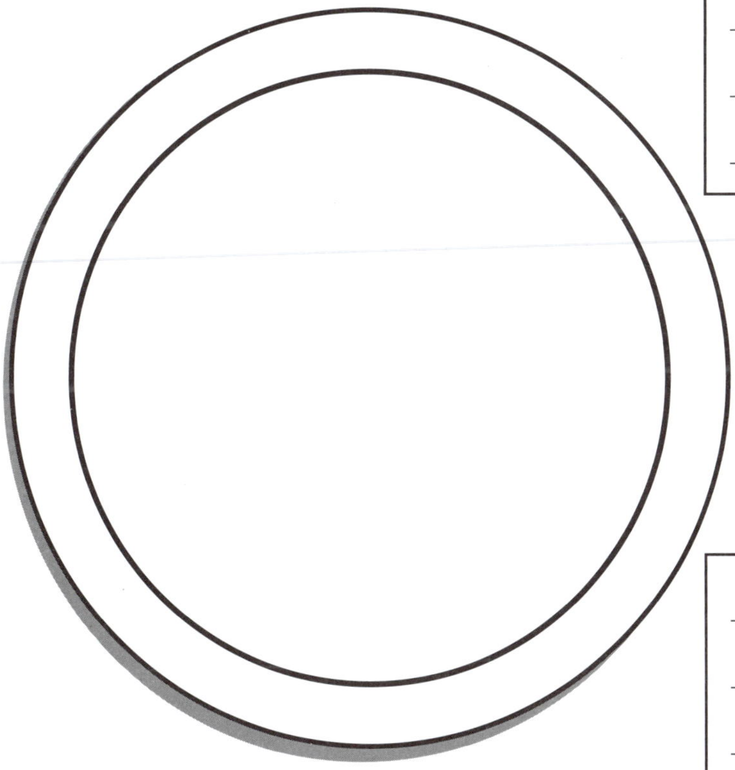

Name: ______________________ Date: ______________

Directions: Closely read these texts. Then, reread "Back of the Cereal Box" on page 23. Complete the chart. Answer the question.

Close-Reading Texts

Cereal: A Popular Food Choice	Healthy Breakfast Choices
Some cereals have lots of sugar, but they do not have many whole grains. Those cereals are not good for you. It is best to choose a cereal that does not have a lot of sugar. Eating too much sugar can be bad for a person's health, and sugar does not provide long-lasting energy for their body.	There are many healthy choices for foods to eat at breakfast. One good choice is eggs. Eggs have a lot of protein, and protein helps bodies grow. Protein is also important for making muscles strong. Protein helps to stop hunger so a person can feel more satisfied when they eat a meal with protein. Some people prefer to eat fresh fruit for breakfast. This can be a good choice as well, but fruit does not have as much protein as eggs. Including fruit is a good way to balance your breakfast.

Ingredients in Healthy Cereals	Ingredients in Unhealthy Cereals

Is Henry's cereal healthy? Explain.

____

____

____

____

____

____

© Shell Education

Name: ______________________ Date: ______________

Directions: Think about the texts from this unit. Then, respond to the prompt.

Imagine one of your friends often skips breakfast. Write a story in which you motivate your friend to eat a healthy breakfast that the two of you create together. Use narrative techniques, such as dialogue and description to tell your story.

© Shell Education

Name: ______________________________ Date: ________________

Directions: Think about what you would put into your own custom-made cereal. Make a cereal box cover for it. Be sure to name your cereal and describe the ingredients.

© Shell Education

Name: ______________________ Date: ______________

Directions: Read the text, and answer the questions.

As You Read

Underline one main idea. Number the details that support it.

Ocean Ecosystems

Oceans cover 71 percent of Earth's surface. Many different ecosystems are found in oceans. An ecosystem is made of living things, including plants and animals. It is also made of nonliving things. These include things such as weather, sunlight, water, and soil.

There are many types of ocean ecosystems. Coral reefs are one example. They are made of dead and living coral. Living corals look like plants. They are actually tiny animals. The reefs provide food and shelter to many organisms. Another ecosystem is the open ocean. This is the top layer of an ocean that is away from the coast. It gets a lot of sunlight. Very large and very small animals live in the open ocean. A final example is the deep-sea layer of the ocean. At this level, there is no sunlight. Not many creatures can live in this bottom layer because it is very cold and dark.

1. Which evidence supports the idea that an ecosystem has nonliving things?
   - (A) They have plants.
   - (B) They have bugs.
   - (C) They have animals.
   - (D) They have weather.

2. What is an *organism*?
   - (A) a tiny plant
   - (B) a large animal
   - (C) any living thing
   - (D) anything that swims

3. Which statement about corals is true?
   - (A) They are tiny plants.
   - (B) They are tiny animals.
   - (C) They harm organisms.
   - (D) They are only in fresh water.

4. Which word uses the same prefix as *percent*?
   - (A) perk
   - (B) pert
   - (C) perilous
   - (D) perennial

Name: ______________________ Date: ______________

Directions: Read the text, and answer the questions.

As You Read

Number the reasons that support the idea that oceans are important.

Ocean Chemistry

The chemistry of oceans is important. There are many things that make up oceans besides water. They are nutrients, salts, and gasses. These all support life in oceans. They are essential to many ocean cycles.

The carbon cycle is one of the ocean's cycles. In it, the surface water absorbs carbon dioxide from the atmosphere. Plants in the water use this carbon dioxide to make food for themselves. And animals in oceans eat those plants. Eventually, the plants and animals die. They sink to the ocean floor. The carbon they had in their bodies goes with them. Places where this occurs are called *carbon sinks*. A carbon sink is anything that absorbs more carbon from the atmosphere than it releases. Carbon sinks are important on Earth. They keep some carbon out of the air, which stops it from making the planet warmer.

part of the carbon cycle

1. Why is the ocean's chemistry important?
   - (A) It supports life.
   - (B) It provides salt.
   - (C) It uses sunlight.
   - (D) It needs nutrients.

2. What is a carbon sink?
   - (A) A place that stores excess carbon.
   - (B) A basin where people can get carbon.
   - (C) An area in the atmosphere that releases carbon.
   - (D) An area of Earth where animals take in carbon.

3. Which word uses the same root word as *atmosphere*?
   - (A) atomic
   - (B) hemisphere
   - (C) shepherd
   - (D) spearhead

4. How do carbon sinks help Earth?
   - (A) They store salt and minerals.
   - (B) They keep land and water plants alive.
   - (C) They help the planet maintain its temperature.
   - (D) They provide nutrients to land and water animals.

© Shell Education

Name: ______________________ Date: ______________

Directions: Read the text, and answer the questions.

As You Read

Circle the two ways oceans are always moving.
Underline details that describe the movements.

Ocean Physics

Currents and waves are two types of ocean movement. Currents happen at the surface. Surface currents bring warm water from the equator toward Earth's poles. These currents are caused by the wind blowing over the top of the water. Currents can also be in deeper water. Deeper currents are slower. These currents start at the poles. There, fresh water from ice and glaciers melt into ocean water. Cold, fresh water is denser than salt water, so it sinks. Once the water sinks, it slowly flows away from the poles into ocean basins. Eventually, this deep water rises. The circulation of currents continues.

Waves are another form of ocean movement. Wind creates waves. Friction from the wind blows against the water's surface, creating waves. Some waves can be caused by storms or earthquakes. Waves created by earthquakes are called *tsunamis*.

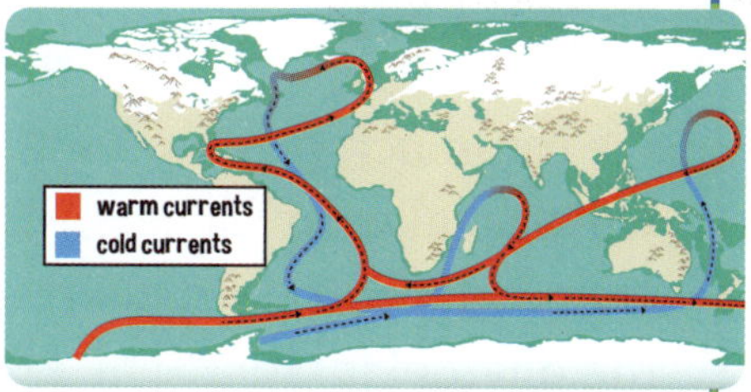

1. What is one main idea of the text?
   - (A) Currents are caused by wind.
   - (B) Currents are one way oceans move.
   - (C) Deep-water currents are slow-moving.
   - (D) Fresh, cold water from the poles sinks.

2. What do both currents and waves have in common?
   - (A) They involve storms.
   - (B) They are caused by wind.
   - (C) They can cause natural disasters.
   - (D) They only happen during certain times of the year.

3. How do surface and deep-water currents work? ______________________

____

4. How can the ocean be both helpful and harmful? ______________________

____

© Shell Education

Name: ____________________ Date: ______________

As You Read

Put a star beside information that describes how algae blooms can be harmful.

Ocean Life: Plankton

Oceans are home to 94 percent of all wildlife on Earth. Of the life in oceans, 90 percent is plankton. The term *plankton* refers to the thousands of small species that are carried by tides and currents. Most of them are microscopically small. There are two types of plankton. The first is phytoplankton. These are plants. The second is zooplankton. These are animals.

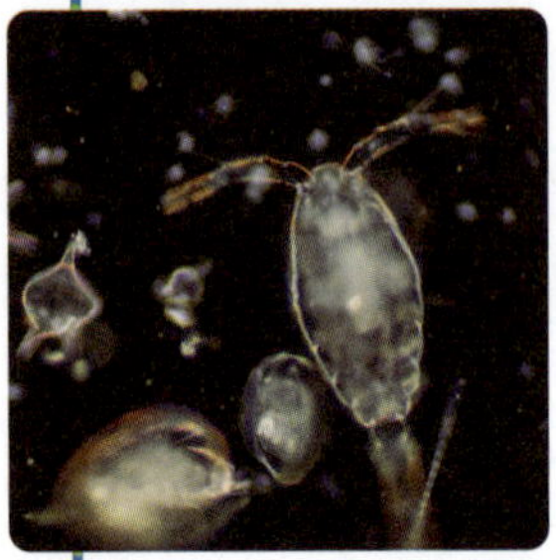

Plankton are important to the health of the planet. Phytoplankton are one of the primary producers of oxygen. They produce over half of all the oxygen on Earth. They form the base of the largest food web in the world. Plankton are necessary for other animals to survive. For example, zooplankton, such as krill, feed on phytoplankton. Larger animals, such as blue whales, feed on krill.

Too much plankton is a bad thing. This is especially true for phytoplankton, which makes up algae. An algal bloom can occur when a large number of algae are produced very quickly. There may be too many nutrients in the water for the phytoplankton. The excess nutrients often come from runoff of stormwater and wastewater. The nutrients could come from agricultural runoff as well, such as fertilizers. Or there may be too much warmth or sunlight hitting the water. Phytoplankton uses photosynthesis, just like plants on land. So, having too much sun and warmth can cause them to grow too quickly.

Algal blooms can be harmful. Sometimes, they block too much sunlight for the water below. This causes the plants and algae below to produce less oxygen. So, there is less oxygen available for animals in the water. The lack of sunlight can also cause plants and algae below the bloom to die. Less plant life in the water means less food for much of the animal life. Animals can begin to die off due to a lack of food and oxygen. If this happens, then nothing in the water usually survives. An area like this, with a lack of life, is known as a dead zone.

Some algae also produce deadly toxins. This act is a defense mechanism. Some algae use this when there are too many algae in an area. These toxins spread into the surrounding area. Animals in the water can get sick. People who consume this water can also get sick. To be safe, people should not go in the water when there is an algal bloom.

© Shell Education

Name: ______________________ Date: ______________

Directions: Read "Ocean Life: Plankton." Then, answer the questions.

1. Why is phytoplankton important?

- (A) They feed most of the ocean's animals.
- (B) They use up excess nutrients in the oceans.
- (C) They produce a majority of Earth's oxygen.
- (D) They use photosynthesis to get rid of excess carbon dioxide.

2. Which is an example of zooplankton?

- (A) algae
- (B) blue whales
- (C) krill
- (D) phytoplankton

3. What is a *defense mechanism*?

- (A) a way to fend off attackers
- (B) an instinct to attack oneself
- (C) a machine that protects living things
- (D) the ability to fight with great strength

4. Which of the following words uses the Greek affix *photo-* similar to its meaning in *photosynthesis*?

- (A) elephoto
- (B) photograph
- (C) photoreg
- (D) synthephoto

5. Write an effect for each cause.

Cause	Effect
A large number of algae are produced very quickly.	
Algal blooms block too much sunlight.	
Algae toxins can spread into surrounding waters.	

© Shell Education

Name: ______________________________ Date: ______________

Directions: Reread the text from this week. Then, respond to the prompt.

Explain how oceans are an important part of Earth. Use facts, definitions, details, quotations, or other examples from the texts to support your ideas.

© Shell Education

Name: ______________________________ Date: ______________

Directions: Read the text, and answer the questions.

As You Read

Place a star beside reasons that explain why being a fish is advantageous.

World Traveler

Traveling around the world was Steve's favorite thing to do. He had seen it all: Europe, South America, even the icebergs in Antarctica. He could go nearly anywhere he wanted, whenever he wanted.

Steve loved the freedom of being a sardine. Of course, he had never been anything else, so he wasn't sure how it measured up to being a shark. He sometimes wished he had their ferocious teeth and aloof attitude. But whenever he felt jealous, he returned to thoughts of his extraordinary travels. His small size and strong fins had allowed him to travel more than most other fish. He had seen plankton, whales, shipwrecks, and even some deep sea creatures. He wished he could go to some of the dead zones, but it was too hard to breathe there.

Steve made many friends during his travels. Sometimes, he would go years without seeing his friends and then pop up out of nowhere for a visit. In fact, that's exactly what he was heading to Australia to do.

1. Which statement is true about Steve?
   - (A) He is a shark.
   - (B) He is a fish.
   - (C) He is a whale.
   - (D) He is a fisherman.

2. Why can't Steve go to dead zones?
   - (A) They don't have water.
   - (B) They don't have plankton.
   - (C) They don't have creatures.
   - (D) They don't have much oxygen.

3. What is an antonym for *extraordinary*?
   - (A) adventurous
   - (B) fascinating
   - (C) normal
   - (D) odd

4. Which prepositional phrase explains *when* Steve traveled?
   - (A) out of nowhere
   - (B) around the world
   - (C) during his travels
   - (D) whenever he wanted

Name: ______________________________ Date: ________________

Directions: Read the text, and answer the questions.

As You Read

Underline ways Steve and Tom are alike. Circle ways they are different.

Greeting an Old Friend

Once Steve began seeing green turtles floating through the water, he knew. Australia was close, and so was Tom, Steve's best friend! Tom was a laid-back Australian sardine who loved science. Tom didn't travel far, but he really knew his way around the Great Barrier Reef. It was Steve's favorite place to visit in Australia.

Steve always knew where to find Tom because of his sedentary nature. He was usually hanging around the clownfish in a shallow part of the reef.

"Steve!" Tom yelled as soon as he spotted him. "How was the journey?"

"Beautiful as always," Steve said, shaking Tom's fin.

"You're just in time," Tom said, swimming excitedly. "The clownfish are going to listen to my jokes and tell me if I'm sharp enough to hit the comedy scene yet."

Steve laughed and happily settled into the audience to listen.

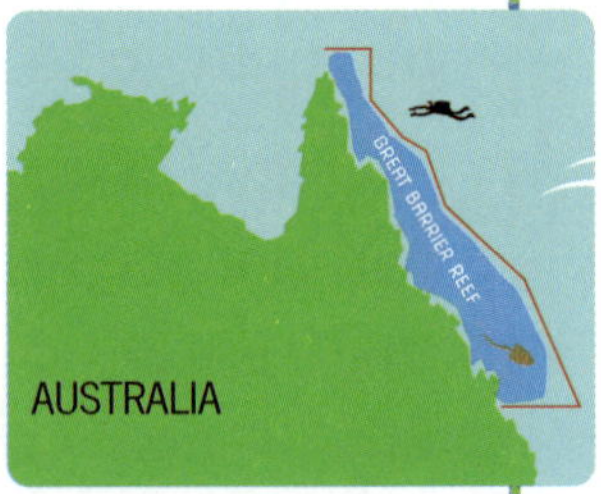

1. How are Steve and Tom different?

Ⓐ Steve stays in one place, but Tom does not.

Ⓑ Steve lives in Australia, but Tom does not.

Ⓒ Steve travels around a lot, but Tom does not.

Ⓓ Tom interacted with other bubbles, but Steve did not.

2. What is the meaning of *sedentary*?

Ⓐ friendly

Ⓑ inactive

Ⓒ mindful

Ⓓ social

3. How are Steve and Tom alike?

Ⓐ They both like the Great Barrier Reef.

Ⓑ They both like being social.

Ⓒ They both live at the Great Barrier Reef.

Ⓓ They both travel a lot.

4. Which best describes Steve and Tom's relationship?

Ⓐ brothers

Ⓑ new friends

Ⓒ enemies

Ⓓ great friends

 © Shell Education

Name: ______________________________ Date: ______________

Directions: Read the text, and answer the questions.

As You Read

Underline facts about the Great Barrier Reef.

Trouble in Paradise

As Steve listened to Tom speak from his coral stage, he looked around the ocean at the Great Barrier Reef. It had always been one of the world's largest underwater capitals. The hustle and bustle of big cities always astounded him.

But then, Steve began to realize something—the corals had changed quite a lot. In his youth, they were stunning, and they contained all the colors you could imagine. But now, the corals on the reef seemed faded. A lot of them were white, and he could tell there weren't as many fish as there used to be.

Steve was finding it hard to laugh at Tom's jokes. He saw a family of hermit crabs loading their supply of shells onto a sea turtle's back and zooming away. Everywhere he looked, he saw families of fish leaving the reef. Steve wasn't sure what was going on, but he was determined to find out.

1. What makes Steve worry?
   - (A) the jokes that Tom tells aren't funny
   - (B) the changes to the Great Barrier Reef
   - (C) the city disappearing
   - (D) he misses his family

2. What does Steve intend to learn?
   - (A) how the Great Barrier Reef has changed and why
   - (B) how coral reefs are related
   - (C) how crabs use shells
   - (D) how the reef compares with the other places he's visited

3. How have the corals changed? ______________________________

____

____

4. What do you think Steve will find out about the coral reef?

____

____

____

Name: ______________________________ Date: ________________

As You Read

Place a star beside the steps to the experiment.

Steve's Big Experiment

"Tom, have you noticed any changes around here?" Steve asked later.

"It's just not how it used to be, mate," Tom sighed. "It's been hotter every year. Some of us are finding it easier to breathe down south, where it's cooler."

"I'll do some research and collect some data," Steve told Tom.

Steve swam around to various parts of the reef to test the water temperatures. He measured the amount of bubbles in the water. He also tested the oxygen levels and took pictures.

It took about a month for him to record all his data. Tom worked with him to summarize his conclusions.

Overall Impressions:

Higher water temperatures were found with fewer healthy coral.

Fewer organisms were found in places with higher temperatures.

Bubble count remained normal in places with higher temperatures.

High temperatures and low oxygen were found with algal blooms.

"This is super detailed," Tom said. "You should share this with my cousin. He works for the National Academy of Bubble Science."

Steve pondered it for a moment and then decided it was a good idea. Something was happening to the Great Barrier Reef. Clearly, they needed to take protective measures before it was too late!

A couple weeks after submitting his paper to the academy, Steve was called in for an appointment. They thanked him for his extensive research and said they were aware of the problem, but they hadn't come up with a solution yet.

"Why not?" Steve asked in surprise.

"Humans are part of the problem," the advisory board told him. "So far, we have not been successful in our communication efforts. We have translation experts, but it has been difficult."

Steve was crestfallen. But then he realized that this was a new research opportunity right in front of him. He was great at communicating.

"I think I may be able to help with that—if you're willing to recruit me," Steve said with a grin.

© Shell Education

Name: ______________________________ Date: ______________

Directions: Read "Steve's Big Experiment." Then, answer the questions.

1. What is Steve's goal?

- (A) to collect data on water temperatures and oxygen levels
- (B) to find ocean water with suitable oxygen levels
- (C) to find new ways to bring more oxygen to the ocean
- (D) to add bubbles to the water around the Great Barrier Reef

2. Why is it important that Steve shares the findings of the experiment?

- (A) so that Steve can boast about his discovery
- (B) so that Tom knows what Steve discovered
- (C) so that other scientists can expand on Steve's work
- (D) so that Steve can explain a complicated idea clearly

3. What is the meaning of *recruit*?

- (A) hire someone
- (B) provide expertise
- (C) replace workers
- (D) write down

4. How does Tom react to Steve's findings?

- (A) He is anxious about them.
- (B) He is excited about them.
- (C) He is indifferent about them.
- (D) He is upset about them.

5. Explain how Steve followed steps of the scientific process.

Research Goal or Question	
Experimental Plan	
Results (list one or two)	
Sharing Data	

Name: ______________________ Date: ____________

Directions: Reread "Steve's Big Experiment." Then, respond to the prompt.

Write a story about an animal who discovers something unusual about their habitat. Use descriptive details and develop a clear sequence of events.

 © Shell Education

Name: ______________________ Date: ______________

Phytoplankton Journal

June 11

Things have been exciting around here lately! It's the beginning of summer, and that means something really awesome has been happening for the last few weeks—it's upwelling time! Water from deep in the ocean has been rising up to the surface and bringing a bunch of nutrients with it. My family and I LOVE nutrients. They are almost all we talk about. Honestly, without nutrients, I wouldn't be here writing this.

With all these nutrients hanging around, and knowing that summer is bringing extra sunlight, we have the perfect setup to form a bloom! I'm so excited because this will be my first time participating in a bloom. My parents have told me what to expect, but I'm still a little nervous. With all the new phytoplankton, what if I get separated from my parents and can't find them? I think I will end up being okay, though.

The coolest part of being part of the bloom is that we can be seen from SPACE! How neat is that? I think I'm going to try to wave at an astronaut. Maybe they'll see me and tell all their friends about it. That would be so cool. Anyway, it's time for me to get some rest in case tomorrow is the big bloom day!

—Al

Name: ______________________________ Date: ______________

Directions: Read "Phytoplankton Journal." Then, answer the questions.

1. What summer event is causing good bloom conditions?
   - (A) colder water
   - (B) new phytoplankton
   - (C) less sunlight
   - (D) upwelling

2. How are the journal writer's emotions reflected in the entry?
   - (A) They use language to express gratitude.
   - (B) The entry is written with formal language.
   - (C) Many sentences end with exclamation points.
   - (D) They describe the sequence of events in great detail.

3. What are *nutrients*?
   - (A) flavors added to foods
   - (B) grasses that grow in the ocean
   - (C) the white and yellow parts of plants
   - (D) things needed for growth and health

4. What is an antonym for *separated*?
   - (A) apart
   - (B) broken
   - (C) mixed up
   - (D) united

5. Would you say the journal writer is more excited or nervous? Explain.

____

____

____

____

____

____

____

____

____

____

____

 © Shell Education

Name: ______________________________ Date: ________________

Directions: Closely read these texts. Then, reread the journal entry on page 41. Check the box or boxes to show which texts have information that support the facts listed.

Close-Reading Texts

Ocean Life: Plankton	World Traveler
An algal bloom can occur when a large number of algae are produced very quickly. There may be too many nutrients in the water for the phytoplankton. The excess nutrients often come from runoff of stormwater and wastewater. The nutrients could come from agricultural runoff as well, such as fertilizers. Or there may be too much warmth or sunlight hitting the water. Phytoplankton uses photosynthesis, just like plants on land. So, having too much sun and warmth can cause them to grow too quickly.	But whenever he felt jealous, he returned to thoughts of his extraordinary travels. His small size and strong fins had allowed him to travel more than most other fish. He had seen plankton, whales, shipwrecks, and even some deep sea creatures. He wished he could go to some of the dead zones, but it was too hard to breathe there.

Facts	Ocean Life: Plankton	World Traveler	Phytoplankton Journal
1. Phytoplankton need sunlight to grow.			
2. Plankton live in the ocean.			
3. Phytoplankton need nutrients to create an algal bloom.			
4. Algal blooms can be seen from space.			
5. Dead zones have little oxygen.			

Name: ______________________________ Date: ______________

Directions: Closely read these texts. Then, compare each character's thought or emotions in response to the events that take place. Explain how you know the characters' thoughts or emotions.

Close-Reading Texts

Steve's Big Experiment	Phytoplankton Journal
"This is super detailed," Tom said, clapping a fin on Steve's back. "You should share this with my cousin. He works for the National Academy of Bubble Science." Steve pondered it for a moment and then decided it was a good idea. Something was happening to the Great Barrier Reef. Clearly, they needed to take protective measures before it was too late!	Things have been exciting around here lately! It's the beginning of summer, and that means something really awesome has been happening for the last few weeks—it's upwelling time! Water from deep in the ocean has been rising up to the surface and bringing a bunch of nutrients with it. My family and I LOVE nutrients. They are almost all we talk about. Honestly, without nutrients, I wouldn't be here writing this.

Character	Response to Events	Evidence
Steve		
Tom		
Phytoplankton		

© Shell Education

Name: ______________________ Date: ______________

Directions: Reread the texts about oceans. Then, respond to the prompt

Explain why you agree or disagree that people should be mindful of ocean pollution. Introduce the topic, state an opinion, and support your opinion with ideas and facts that support your ideas.

© Shell Education

Name: ______________________________ Date: ______________

Directions: Write the phytoplankton's next journal entry. Describe what happens during the bloom. Use descriptive words and phrases and sensory details to explain the events.

© Shell Education

Name: ______________________ Date: ______________

Directions: Read the text, and answer the questions.

As You Read

Underline different types of stores you may find in malls. Place a star by your favorite one.

All about Malls

Malls are large, convenient areas with a variety of stores. People can purchase clothes, shoes, books, and computers all in the same place. Malls often have many interesting restaurants, too.

Most malls have large department stores called *anchor stores*. These anchor stores are typically the main stores in a mall. Malls also have smaller stores that sell different types of products. For example, jewelry stores, video game stores, and gift shops are a few of the types of stores that can be found in malls.

Malls have other places that sell items and services, too. One example is kiosks (KEE-ahsks). Kiosks are small stands that are placed around the mall. Kiosks sell many different things, including hats, stuffed animals, watches, and T-shirts. Many malls also have beauty salons, barbers, and eyeglasses stores. Plus, you can't forget the food court! Most malls have one area for fast-food options. Kiosks can sell food, such as cookies or hot dogs, too.

1. What is the main idea?

- (A) Anchor stores are large department stores.
- (B) Gift shops are smaller stores.
- (C) Kiosks are small stands.
- (D) Malls are convenient places where people can shop.

2. What are the main stores in many malls called?

- (A) anchor stores
- (B) gift shops
- (C) kiosks
- (D) malls

3. How does a kiosk compare to an anchor store?

- (A) A kiosk is bigger.
- (B) A kiosk is smaller.
- (C) A kiosk is an anchor store.
- (D) A kiosk sells expensive items.

4. What could be described as *convenient*?

- (A) a six-page menu
- (B) a line at the post office
- (C) a commercial on television
- (D) a drive-through window at a restaurant

Name: ______________________ Date: ____________

Directions: Read the text, and answer the questions.

As You Read

Place a star beside facts that explain why people built malls.

The History of Malls

There are many malls in the United States today, but this wasn't always true. Many years ago, most stores were in downtown areas in the main part of a city. But in the early 1950s, many people began to move out of cities. They moved to suburbs, which are smaller towns near cities. Those people wanted to have stores near them, and they did not want to take long trips into the city to go shopping. Many malls were built so that people could shop near their homes. The idea of a mall was to have many stores under one roof so that people would want to spend more time shopping. And because malls were covered, people could get their shopping done even if it was cold or raining. By the 1980s, malls were so popular that they became social gathering places for people.

1. According to this text, why were malls built?
   - (A) so people could go to the movies
   - (B) so people could move out of the cities
   - (C) so people could go downtown to shop
   - (D) so people could shop near their homes

2. In which of the following words does the Latin root *sub-* have a similar meaning to *suburb*?
   - (A) subject
   - (B) submarine
   - (C) substance
   - (D) subtle

3. According to this text, how have malls changed since they were first built?
   - (A) Malls now have food courts.
   - (B) Stores in malls are larger.
   - (C) People use them as places to get together.
   - (D) Construction materials have become stronger.

4. What does the phrase *under one roof* mean?
   - (A) a flat roof
   - (B) more than one building
   - (C) a roof made of one material
   - (D) different things in one place

 © Shell Education

Name: ______________________ Date: ______________

Directions: Read the text, and answer the questions.

As You Read

Circle key words that tell how malls are different today.

Modern Malls

Malls are still popular, but they may not be as busy as they once were. This is because people now have other ways to shop. People don't have to go to malls to find what they want because they can shop online. So, malls try to offer things that people cannot find online. Many malls offer entertainment or fun activities for people to do. For example, some malls have movie theaters and bowling alleys. Many malls have play areas for children, and some malls even have roller coasters! Other malls offer fitness centers and doctors' offices. Some malls were designed to be outdoor malls. This allows people to have more options for shopping, eating, and gathering.

roller coasters in the Mall of America, Minnesota

Malls have changed a great deal since they were first built in the 1950s. But they are still important parts of many people's lives. They can be good places to shop for almost anything and meet with friends.

1. Which is one reason why malls have changed?
   - (A) People can meet with friends.
   - (B) Malls have movie theaters.
   - (C) People can find what they want online.
   - (D) Malls have gotten busier.

2. Which of these means *fun things to do*?
   - (A) gathering
   - (B) bowling
   - (C) entertainment
   - (D) fitness centers

3. What is one main idea of this text? ______________________________

____

4. Do you think malls have improved over time? Explain your opinion.

____

____

Name: ____________________ Date: ____________

As You Read

Circle three facts about the Mall of America.
Underline three facts about the Dubai Mall.

A World of Shopping

Some malls are much larger than other malls. A few malls are so big that they almost seem like cities. The largest mall in the world is in Dubai, which is a city in the United Arab Emirates. Another large mall is the Mall of America near St. Paul, Minnesota. About 32 large airplanes could fit inside! Both of these malls have many things for people to see and do.

Dubai, United Arab Emirates

The Mall of America has many fun attractions for people. There is a flight simulator, a mirror maze, and a miniature golf course. This mall has a huge aquarium, too. And it even has a full-size theme park. You'll find a movie theater there, too. It has 14 screens.

Of course, people can also shop at the Mall of America. There are more than 520 stores at the mall. They sell everything from clothes and jewelry to groceries. At one store, you can make your own stuffed bear! If you spent just 10 minutes at each store at the Mall of America, it would take you 86 hours to see each one. That's more than three days!

The Dubai Mall has twice as many stores as the Mall of America. In total, it has over 1,200 stores. It also has a skating rink and a large movie theater. There is an aquarium, too!

If you're hungry, the Dubai Mall has over 200 restaurants. Some are fast-food restaurants, and some are fancy restaurants. There are family restaurants at the mall, too. After you eat, you can shop for anything you might want.

The Dubai Mall is so big that you cannot visit the whole mall in one day. So, there is a hotel connected to the mall. People who want to spend several days visiting the mall can stay at that hotel.

There are countless options for shopping and entertainment at malls around the world. Some of the largest malls, including the Mall of America and the Dubai Mall, provide even more fun for everyone!

© Shell Education

Name: ______________________ Date: ____________

Directions: Read "A World of Shopping." Then, answer the questions.

1. Why did the author write this text?
   - (A) to give directions to the Mall of America
   - (B) to tell about two of the world's largest malls
   - (C) to tell readers how to be safe when shopping at the mall
   - (D) to get readers to visit the aquarium at the Mall of America

2. Which of these similes may be best used to describe both malls?
   - (A) bright as a button
   - (B) busy as a bee
   - (C) cold as ice
   - (D) quiet as a mouse

3. What can you do in a flight simulator?
   - (A) pretend to fly an airplane
   - (B) build and fly paper airplanes
   - (C) see replicas of famous airplanes
   - (D) feel the wind against an airplane in flight

4. Which pair of words correctly compares the structure of this text to "The History of Malls"?
   - (A) compare-contrast; problem-solution
   - (B) chronological order; compare-contrast
   - (C) cause-effect; chronological order
   - (D) problem-solution; cause-effect

5. Compare and contrast the Mall of America to the Dubai Mall.

The Mall of America	**The Dubai Mall**
Both	

UNIT 3
WEEK 1
DAY
5

Name: ______________________ Date: ______________

Directions: Reread "A World of Shopping." Then, respond to the prompt.

Imagine you are at one of these two malls for one day. Make a plan for your day. What would you do? Write about how you would spend your day.

© Shell Education

Name: ______________________________ Date: ______________

Directions: Read the text, and answer the questions.

As You Read

Place exclamation points (!) beside events that surprise you.

Mystery Box

Jazmine and her sister Elizabeth were going back-to-school shopping at the mall with their mom. They both wanted to be browsing the shelves of new video games at Game On, not looking for new clothes. After hitting two stores, they convinced their mom to let them have a 15-minute break. Their mom went to find a pretzel, and they went to find something more exciting to do.

After walking toward the end of one side of the mall, Elizabeth pointed at a large, black box in the middle of the walking path.

"What is that?" she asked. "I've never seen anything like that before."

The box was about the size of a kiosk, and at the front, there was a door with a QR code on it. Jasmine scanned the QR code, and it took her to a website that simply read, *Enter*. The girls shrugged at each other and went inside the box.

Inside, a huge white screen was mounted on the wall in front of the couch. The lights dimmed. The word *welcome* slowly appeared across the screen.

1. Jazmine and Elizabeth are both ______.
   - Ⓐ boring
   - Ⓑ curious
   - Ⓒ scared
   - Ⓓ friendly

2. Why do Jazmine and Elizabeth leave their mom?
   - Ⓐ They do not like to shop for clothes.
   - Ⓑ They want to find an adventure.
   - Ⓒ They are meeting friends.
   - Ⓓ They are heading toward the food court.

3. What might Jazmine most likely use to scan the QR code?
   - Ⓐ a laptop
   - Ⓑ her cell phone
   - Ⓒ a digital camera
   - Ⓓ an instant camera

4. What happens to the lights inside the room?
   - Ⓐ They brighten.
   - Ⓑ They flicker.
   - Ⓒ They lower.
   - Ⓓ They go out.

Name: ____________________ Date: ____________

Directions: Read the text, and answer the questions.

As You Read

Circle words that describe how the girls feel.

A Strange Introduction

Jazmine and Elizabeth continued to watch the screen. Then, something began to happen. A deep, atmospheric hum was the only sound they could initially hear. The sounds became lighter, and the screen filled with images of bright stars and galaxies.

They soon started to feel mesmerized and excited as the swirling galaxies began to race by faster and faster. The music was picking up speed, too. Soon, the screen was a blur of colorful light.

"It's going at warp speed or something," Elizabeth said, in awe of the screen. Both girls stared at the rushing colors, starting to feel dizzy.

The box began to shake. Jazmine and Elizbeth looked toward each other, unsure of what was happening or what to do.

1. How do the girls' feelings change?
   - (A) first curious, then excited, then unsure
   - (B) first excited, then unsure, then curious
   - (C) first curious, then unsure, then excited
   - (D) first unsure, then curious, then excited

2. How do the galaxies change when the music changes?
   - (A) They move more quickly.
   - (B) They vibrate and move.
   - (C) They disappear from the screen.
   - (D) They move in a square.

3. What might the *atmospheric hum* sound like?
   - (A) a crash like musical cymbals
   - (B) a high-pitched squeal like a whale call
   - (C) a car squealing to a halt
   - (D) the rumbling of a jet engine

4. What is a synonym for *mesmerized*?
   - (A) bewildered
   - (B) entranced
   - (C) indifferent
   - (D) steady

 © Shell Education

Name: ______________________________ Date: ______________

Directions: Read the text, and answer the questions.

As You Read

Underline the part(s) of the text that explain when the girls' feelings change.

A Stranger End

The box continued shaking, and the music got even louder. It almost hurt Elizabeth's ears! Then, the galaxies on the screen stopped rushing by. Six of them appeared on screen. They began to flash in a pattern of rainbow colors, and the music slowed down to a ticking clock noise.

"What's happening now?" Elizabeth asked.

"Oh, maybe I can check the QR code," Jazmine said. She pulled up the webpage again and saw that a countdown had appeared, and it was counting down from 30 seconds. She showed Elizabeth the screen and smiled with relief.

"I guess that means it's almost over," she said, happily. "I wanted an adventure, but I'm not sure how I felt about that."

"Yeah, it was weird—but kind of cool too though, right?" Elizabeth asked.

1. How does the music change?
   - (A) It gets softer and turns into a clock noise.
   - (B) It gets louder and turns into a clock noise.
   - (C) It gets louder and faster.
   - (D) It gets lower-pitched.

2. Why does Jazmine go to the website again?
   - (A) She thinks it will explain things.
   - (B) She thinks it will show cool images.
   - (C) She thinks it willl allow her to send a message.
   - (D) She thinks it will let her report where they were.

3. Why is Jazmine relieved when she sees a countdown? ______________________

   ____

4. Why do you think the girls laugh? ______________________________

   ____

Name: ______________________________ Date: ________________

As You Read

Underline words or phrases that tell about what the girls think or feel.

Quite a Trip

Jazmine and Elizabeth were relieved to step outside the box. They immediately hurried toward the food court to find their mom, but they soon realized that the mall they were in was completely different. They didn't even see the food court!

Jazmine decided they should go back to the box to investigate. Next to the box was an information panel with these words printed at the top: *The Florence Mall.* "Where is the Florence Mall?" Elizabeth asked.

"No idea," Jazmine answered. "I think we should get back in the box."

The girls sat on the couch and thought for a moment. Jazmine decided to go back to the website the QR code had taken her to. After she tapped the bottom right corner, a settings menu popped up.

"Nice job!" Elizabeth said. Jazmine scrolled down and clicked on the word *destination.*

A voice said, "Welcome to the Magic Mall Box. Please select a destination."

Both girls gasped. They looked at Jazmine's phone and saw a list of malls. Jazmine selected the mall they came from. The box shook, and then it stopped.

The girls stepped outside the box and realized they were at the right place. They ran to the food court and saw their mom just sitting down to eat a pretzel.

"You're done already?" she asked. "I was thinking of getting a lemonade, but if you're ready, I can—"

"Oh no, we just wanted to say…" Elizabeth said, trailing off.

"Thanks for taking us to the mall!" Jazmine said. The girls waved at their mom and quickly ran back to the black box. They nodded at each other and Jazmine selected another destination from her screen.

The girls visited the Dubai Mall and the Mall of America. They saw a mall in Alberta, Canada, and one mall in Doha, Qatar. They rode rollercoasters and saw a beautiful aquarium. When they were exhausted, they finally went back home.

They found their mom at the food court, enjoying her lemonade and pretzel.

"Did you find anything exciting?" their mom asked them.

The girls smiled at each other and laughed. They could only hope that next year's back-to-school shopping trip would be this fun!

© Shell Education

Name: ______________________________ Date: ______________

Directions: Read "Quite a Trip." Then, answer the questions.

1. How do the girls begin to know they are in a different mall?
   - Ⓐ The box disappears.
   - Ⓑ The stores are different.
   - Ⓒ Their friends aren't there.
   - Ⓓ The food court is in a different place.

2. What is the best reason to explain why the girls return to the box so quickly?
   - Ⓐ They feel safe there.
   - Ⓑ They want to hide.
   - Ⓒ They need time to plan their escape.
   - Ⓓ They do not feel like exploring a new place.

3. What is something a person might *investigate*?
   - Ⓐ a family recipe
   - Ⓑ a home computer
   - Ⓒ a new walking trail
   - Ⓓ a well-planned travel route

4. Why do the girls go to all those other malls?
   - Ⓐ to be adventurous
   - Ⓑ to be creative
   - Ⓒ to be stubborn
   - Ⓓ to be troublemakers

5. Explain how the characters show each trait.

Traits	Actions to Demonstrate
clever	
adventurous	
hopeful	

Name: ______________________________ Date: ______________

Directions: Reread "A Quick Trip." Then, respond to the prompt.

Write a story about a time when you found something strange at a mall. Use descriptive words and phrases and sensory details to tell your story.

© Shell Education

Name: ______________________ Date: ______________

Malls Around the World

Mall of America

Location: Bloomington, Minnesota

Facts

- opened in 1992
- largest mall in the United States
- has over 520 stores
- houses an indoor theme park that includes roller coasters and a miniature golf course
- has been used as a filming location for numerous movies and TV shows

Iran Mall

Location: Tehran, Iran

Facts

- largest shopping mall in the world in terms of area
- houses over 700 shops
- contains a hotel, a multiplex cinema, an ice rink, and a bowling alley

Dubai Mall

Location: Dubai, United Arab Emirates

Facts

- second-largest mall in the world by land area after the Iran Mall
- the most visited building on Earth in 2011 with 54 million visitors
- houses the Dubai Aquarium, the world's largest indoor aquarium

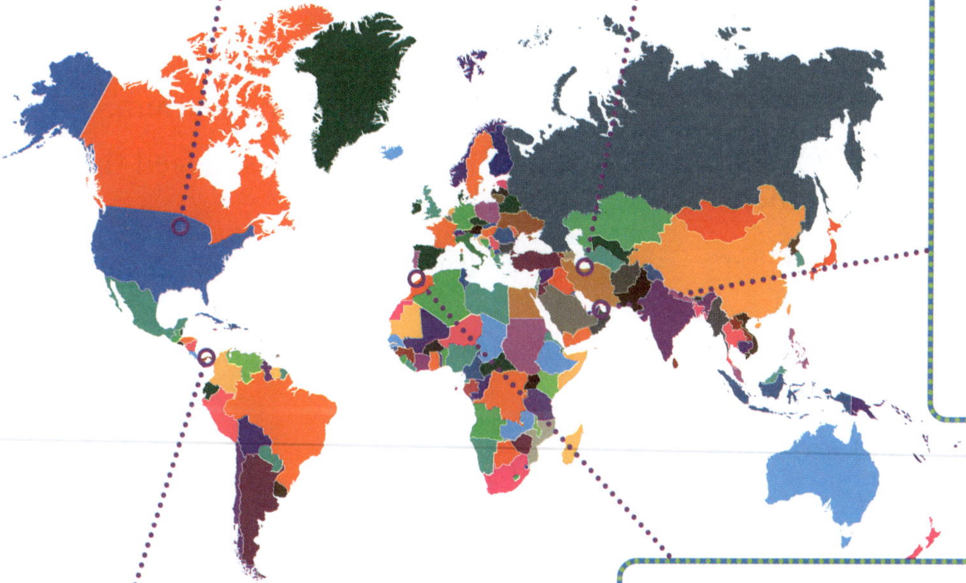

Albrook Mall

Location: Panama City, Panama

Facts

- largest mall in Latin America
- 25th largest mall in the world
- has around 700 stores

Morocco Mall

Location: Casablanca, Morocco

Facts

- largest mall in Africa
- home to a large aquarium called *Aquadream* with more than 40 different species of fish
- The aquarium is a cylinder with an open center. Visitors are able to take an elevator ride through the center that allows for a 360-degree view of the fish.

© Shell Education

Name: ______________________________ Date: ______________

Directions: Read "Malls Around the World." Then, answer the questions.

1. How are the sections of the text related?
   - (A) They describe malls around the world.
   - (B) They tell how malls around the world are safe.
   - (C) They explain how many people visit malls around the world each year.
   - (D) They describe how malls around the world were built.

2. How does the map support the information in the text?
   - (A) It shows the location of each mall.
   - (B) It shows how far away the malls are from each other.
   - (C) It shows where the malls are on each of the seven continents.
   - (D) It shows how people can travel to get to the malls around the world.

3. What can you infer about the Dubai Mall?
   - (A) It took longer to build than any other mall.
   - (B) People come from all over the world to see it.
   - (C) It is located in an area far away from a big city.
   - (D) People have to pay to park in the mall parking lot.

4. What is unique about the aquarium in the Morocco Mall?
   - (A) It is free.
   - (B) It has more species of fish than any other aquarium.
   - (C) It allows visitors to feed the fish.
   - (D) It is shaped like a soup can.

5. Which mall seems the most interesting to you? Explain why.

____

____

____

____

____

© Shell Education

Name: ______________________________ Date: ________________

Directions: Closely read these texts. Then, reread *Malls Around the World* on page 59. Integrate information from all three texts to list details that support the main ideas.

Close-Reading Texts

A World of Shopping	Quite a Trip
If you're hungry, the Dubai Mall has over 200 restaurants. Some are fast-food restaurants, and some are fancy restaurants. There are family restaurants at the mall, too. After you eat, you can shop for anything you might want.	It was a whirlwind of an afternoon. The girls visited the Dubai Mall and the Mall of America. They even went outside of the United States and saw a mall in Alberta, Canada, and one mall in Doha, Qatar. They rode rollercoasters and saw a beautiful aquarium. When they were exhausted, they finally went back home.

Malls are not just for shopping anymore.

There is a little something for everyone at malls.

Name: ______________________ Date: ______________

Directions: Closely read these texts. Then, compare and contrast shopping before and after malls were built.

Close-Reading Texts

History of Malls	Malls
There are many malls in the United States today, but this wasn't always true. Many years ago, most stores were in downtown areas in the main part of a city. But in the early 1950s, many people began to move out of cities. They moved to suburbs, which are smaller towns near cities. Those people wanted to have stores near them, and they did not want to take long trips into the city to go shopping.	Most malls have large department stores called *anchor stores*. These anchor stores are typically the main stores in a mall. Malls also have smaller stores that usually sell different types of products. For example, jewelry stores, video game stores, and gift shops are just a few of the types of stores that can be found in malls. Malls have other places that sell items and services, too. One example is kiosks (KEE-ahsks). Kiosks are small stands that are often placed in the middle of a mall.

Before Malls Were Built	After Malls Were Built

Both

 © Shell Education

Name: ______________________________ Date: ______________

Directions: Think about the texts from this unit. Then, respond to the prompt.

Choose a mall you would like to visit. Write a letter to convince your family that they should take a trip to this mall. Provide logically ordered reasons that are supported by facts and details.

© Shell Education

Name: ______________________________ Date: ______________

Directions: Use what you learned about malls. Learn about a mall near you. Make a fact sheet about it.

Name: ______________________________

Location: ______________________________

Facts: ______________________________

____

____

____

____

____

____

 © Shell Education

Name: ______________________ Date: ____________

Directions: Read the text, and answer the questions.

As You Read

Underline and number the reasons the author gives for why people like pizza.

Pizza Is Popular!

Is pizza one of your favorite foods? If it is, you're not alone. Every year, about three billion pizzas are sold in the United States. And data shows that children like pizza more than any other type of food. For lunch or dinner, children would rather eat pizza than anything else.

There are many reasons why people love pizza so much. One reason is that pizza is easy to eat. It doesn't require a knife or fork; you can simply eat it with your hands. There are also many options for types of pizza. The base ingredients are a crust, sauce, and toppings, and the sky's the limit when it comes to what you can have on it! Some people are happy to enjoy a plain cheese pizza, while other people love adding as many veggies as possible on top. There is also a popular debate: does pineapple belong on pizza? Finally, pizza is also inexpensive. You can have a very tasty meal without spending a lot of money!

1. According to the author, what is one reason people love pizza?
   - (A) Pizza is easy to eat.
   - (B) Pizza is healthy.
   - (C) Pizza is small.
   - (D) Pizza is spicy.

2. Some people may describe pizza as *scrumptious*. What does *scrumptious* mean?
   - (A) inexpensive
   - (B) popular
   - (C) round
   - (D) tasty

3. What is one main idea of the text?
   - (A) Pizza is inexpensive.
   - (B) Pizza is loved by children.
   - (C) Pizza is popular for many reasons.
   - (D) Pizza can be eaten without a knife or fork.

4. Which simile best describes the topic of this text?
   - (A) as long as a snake
   - (B) as tasty as pie
   - (C) wet like the rain
   - (D) as dry as the desert

Name: ______________________ Date: ______________

Directions: Read the text, and answer the questions.

As You Read

Circle the names of different groups of people who are part of the history of pizza making.

The History of Pizza

Pizza has been around for longer than you might think. People in ancient Egypt and Greece used to eat flat bread covered with olive oil and other toppings. In Italy, people in the past baked bread under hot stones. Then, they topped the bread with spices and other ingredients.

The pizza people eat today was created in 1889. It was made by Raffaele Esposito in Naples, Italy. He made a pizza to honor a visiting king and queen.

It took a while for pizza to become popular in the United States. Some Italians moved to the United States in the late 1800s. They brought pizza with them. But most people did not know about it. Pizza became popular in the United States after World War II. American soldiers ate pizza in Italy. When they came home from the war, they wanted pizza at home. More and more people started eating pizza!

1. Which event happened first?
   - (A) Pizza came to the United States.
   - (B) Early Italians baked bread under hot stones.
   - (C) Pizza became popular all over the United States.
   - (D) Raffaele Esposito made pizza for a king and queen.

2. Which phrase describes *when* pizza became popular in the U.S.?
   - (A) after World War II
   - (B) during the 1800s
   - (C) for a long time
   - (D) under hot stones

3. What does *ancient* mean?
   - (A) tropical
   - (B) present-day
   - (C) very nervous
   - (D) long, long ago

4. Which idea is supported in this text and in "Pizza Is Popular!"?
   - (A) People enjoy eating pizza.
   - (B) Pizza is the food of royalty.
   - (C) People don't put different toppings on pizza.
   - (D) Pizza is more popular in Italy than in the United States.

 © Shell Education

Name: ______________________ Date: ____________

Directions: Read the text, and answer the questions.

As You Read

Circle words that indicate time-order events.

How to Make Pizza

A chef will follow several steps while making pizza. First, the chef will begin by mixing the ingredients for pizza dough, such as flour, yeast, and water. After the dough is mixed, the chef lets the dough rise. Then, it is rolled flat. Most pizzas are circular, but some pizzas look like squares or rectangles. Then, the chef spreads some sauce on the dough. There are several different kinds of sauce options, such as tomato sauce, garlic sauce, or barbecue sauce. Next, the chef adds the toppings and the cheese. When the ingredients have been put together, the chef puts the pizza into a special pan. Then, the chef uses a tool called a *paddle* to put the pizza into an oven. When the pizza is cooked through, the chef pulls it out, and they set it on a counter. They use a pizza cutter to make slices in the pizza, and the pizza is now ready for people to enjoy!

1. What does a chef do right after adding the toppings and cheese?
   - (A) adds more toppings
   - (B) put the pizza into a special pizza pan
   - (C) mixes ingredients for the pizza dough
   - (D) spreads some tomato sauce on the dough

2. Which of the following is **not** listed as an ingredient of pizza?
   - (A) baking soda
   - (B) flour
   - (C) water
   - (D) yeast

3. Which tools do chefs use to make pizza? ______________________

____

4. Which toppings do you like on your pizza? ______________________

____

Name: ______________________ Date: ______________

As You Read

Underline or circle ingredients found on different pizzas around the world.

We Love Pizza!

Pizza is very popular all around the world. People from many different countries love to eat it. And in each country, the pizza is slightly different.

In Japan, for instance, there are two main styles of pizza. One kind looks like the pizza you can get in the United States, but it often has seafood on it. The other kind of Japanese pizza looks more like a pancake. The ingredients in that pizza are mixed up into the batter. Then, the batter is cooked like a pancake. Finally, the pizza is cut into slices and served hot and fresh.

Many people in India also eat pizza. Pizza crust in India is often served on a type of bread called naan (NAHN). It is a thin, chewy dough that is often brushed with butter and garlic. In India, you can get pizza with pepperoni on it. You can also get pizza topped with tandoori chicken. This is a special type of grilled chicken. Or you can get your pizza with tofu on it, too. Some Indians also add chili flakes and ketchup to their pizza.

Australians also love pizza. If you go to Australia, you can get a pizza with pepperoni. But you can also get a pizza with lamb or eggs on it. Just like in the United States, you can get a pizza with ham and pineapple. Pineapple is the most popular pizza topping in Australia. Some Australians also like cut-up pumpkin on their pizza. Other Australians like shrimp on their pizza.

Around the world, the options are limitless for what people can put on their pizzas. If you can imagine a pizza, you can probably create it! What toppings do you like on your pizza? Chances are, someone else in the world also likes that type of pizza!

 © Shell Education

Name: ______________________ Date: ______________

Directions: Read “We Love Pizza!” Then, answer the questions.

1. What is one main idea of this text?
   - (A) Pizza is a popular food choice in the United States.
   - (B) People of different countries make pizza differently.
   - (C) Pizza is an unhealthy food choice around the world.
   - (D) People in different parts of the world do not eat pizza.

2. What is true about pizza in both India and Australia?
   - (A) You can get pizza with lamb.
   - (B) You can get pizza with pumpkin.
   - (C) You can get pizza with pepperoni.
   - (D) You can get pizza with tandoori chicken.

3. The author writes, “If you can imagine a pizza, you can probably create it!” Why did the author most likely end this statement with an exclamation point?
   - (A) to show anxiety
   - (B) to show excitement
   - (C) to show confusion
   - (D) to show thankfulness

4. Which pair of words correctly compares the structure of this text to “How to Make Pizza”?
   - (A) cause-effect; problem-solution
   - (B) problem-solution; cause-effect
   - (C) compare-contrast; chronological order
   - (D) chronological order; compare-contrast

5. List unique ingredients found on pizza from each country.

Country	Japan	India	Australia
Ingredients			

Name: ______________________________ Date: ______________

Directions: Reread "We Love Pizza!" Then, respond to the prompt.

Which pizza from the text would you be most interested in eating? State your opinion and support your idea using reasons, facts, and details.

 © Shell Education

Name: ______________________________ Date: ______________

Directions: Read the text, and answer the questions.

As You Read

Number the ideas Kevin shares about his future jobs.

When I Grow Up

At school, Kevin's teacher handed out papers. Kevin slid down in his chair. Writing was one of his least favorite parts of school. But when he turned his paper over and saw the prompt on the front, he got excited.

The prompt read: *What do you want to do when you grow up?*

He put his pencil to the paper, and the words came to him easily:

When I grow up, I mostly want to be a chef, and I would like to be chef who makes delicious pizzas. My family and I have always loved pizza, and there are so many kinds to make. Sometimes, I also think it would be cool to be an astronaut because I love space. Another thing I would like to be is an actor. I love going to see movies with my dad, and sometimes I even like to do my own impressions.

1. What reason does Kevin give for wanting to be an actor?
   - (A) He wants to be famous.
   - (B) He likes to read lines.
   - (C) He wants his dad to be proud of him.
   - (D) He enjoys movies and acting like the actors.

2. How does Kevin feel about pizza?
   - (A) He wants to make anything but pizza.
   - (B) He loves the variety pizza can have.
   - (C) He does not like it.
   - (D) He thinks it's just okay.

3. What are *impressions*?
   - (A) people's personalities
   - (B) made-up stories
   - (C) imitating someone else
   - (D) feelings people have

4. Why is there a comma after the phrase, *When I grow up,*?
   - (A) It tells the reader that someone is speaking.
   - (B) It tells the reader that the sentence is complete.
   - (C) It separates an introductory clause from the sentence.
   - (D) It gives the reader time to breathe when reading a long sentence.

Name: ______________________ Date: ______________

Directions: Read the text, and answer the questions.

As You Read

Circle the item that piques Kevin's interest. Underline details about the item.

A Family Tradition

The next morning, Kevin told his dad about the journal prompt from school.

"I'm going to let you in on a little family secret," he said, walking over to one of the kitchen cabinets. He grabbed a large binder and set it down on the counter.

"What is that?" Kevin asked, staring at the massive binder.

"It's our trusty family recipe book," his dad said. "You know how we make pizzas for our family dinner every month? All the recipes we use come from this."

"But you never look at the book," Kevin said, confused. His dad laughed and explained that he'd been using them for so long that he'd memorized them.

Kevin looked through the recipe book while he finished eating his breakfast. He noticed that some recipes were half-finished and some recipes were so tattered that they were barely readable. Then, he saw a pizza recipe that really caught his eye.

"Dad, I think I have an idea for the next family pizza," Kevin said.

"We'll make whichever pizza you've picked!" his dad exclaimed.

1. Where does this part of the story take place?
   - (A) at Kevin's house in the den
   - (B) in Kevin's classroom
   - (C) at a pizza restaurant
   - (D) in Kevin's kitchen

2. What is wrong with some of the family recipes?
   - (A) They aren't exactly complete.
   - (B) They list the wrong ingredients.
   - (C) They haven't been tried in many years.
   - (D) They are removed from the recipe book.

3. What is an antonym for *massive*?
   - (A) bulky
   - (B) immense
   - (C) thorough
   - (D) tiny

4. What do Kevin and his dad have in common?
   - (A) They both enjoy pizza.
   - (B) They both enjoy coffee.
   - (C) They both enjoy journals.
   - (D) They both enjoy writing recipes.

 © Shell Education

Name: ______________________________ Date: ______________

Directions: Read the text, and answer the questions.

As You Read

Place a star beside the challenge Kevin gives himself.

Kevin's Pizzeria

Kevin wanted to get some practice making pizza before he had to make it for his whole family. So, he decided to keep trying different recipes. First, he had to figure out how to make a pizza dough. It took him several attempts and a lot of help from his dad, but Kevin finally got it. He also added a secret ingredient to the dough, which was a few shakes of Italian seasoning.

After Kevin's mom and dad raved about his practice pizza, he decided to make a plan. He wanted to make every pizza recipe in the book. He even wanted to make the ones that had missing parts.

The kitchen became a pizza parlor over the next week. His dad started to call the kitchen "Kevin's Pizzeria." Kevin's mom customized a sign for it. She printed the words and hung it up across the kitchen door. Kevin loved it!

1. What does Kevin challenge himself to do?

- (A) turn his kitchen into a pizza parlor
- (B) improve the recipes
- (C) make every pizza recipe in the family recipe book
- (D) write down more recipes in the family recipe book

2. What is something that may be *customized*?

- (A) a blender
- (B) a coffee mug
- (C) a pack of lined paper
- (D) a puppy

3. How does Kevin's whole family get involved in his pizza-making?

____

____

4. What character traits does Kevin reveal through his actions?

____

Name: ________________________________ Date: ______________

As You Read

Place a *C* beside one or more causes. Place an *E* beside the effect(s) of the cause(s).

Cooking Competition

Kevin continued to work on his pizza-making skills. When it came time for the family pizza night, he knocked it out of the park! After that night, he kept making pizzas. He was having so much fun with the family recipe book. For dessert one night, he made sweet cinnamon knots out of leftover pizza dough. Then, he made a breakfast pizza with ham, spinach, and a fried egg on top!

"Kevin, this is amazing," his dad said, finishing up a slice. "Have you ever thought about entering a cooking competition?"

"I've thought about opening a pizza restaurant," Kevin told his parents. "But I guess entering a competition seems like a better first step."

Kevin and his parents found a kids-only cooking competition. Everyone had to make a "comfort food" dish. Kevin was excited to enter, but he also felt nervous.

Kevin decided to focus on his pizza recipe instead of worrying. It was one of the recipes that was half-finished, so Kevin had to fill in the gaps. He made some mistakes each time he practiced, but he felt it turned out great each time.

The morning of the competition, Kevin headed to the center with his dad. Every child who was entering had to have an adult with them. The adult could help with tasks, such as chopping vegetables, but they couldn't participate in the actual cooking.

Kevin and his dad set to work making the pizza. His dad chopped basil for him, and Kevin pulled the sauce and dough together. Measuring out the ingredients for the sauce was the most complicated part. It involved using a variety of fresh garlic, basil, and crushed tomatoes. He also had to use extra virgin olive oil, some salt and pepper, and oregano. He put everything into a bowl and mixed it well.

His pizza came out of the oven with a crisp crust. And it was perfectly gooey and cheesy. At tasting time, the judges praised him for taking a simple recipe and making it well. Some judges even said it was the best dish they had eaten all night!

"It would be perfect in my eyes," said the last judge, "but I think the sauce has a bit too much garlic."

Kevin smiled and made a mental note to update the recipe book when he got home. He was proud of how well he had done, and he was happy to be one step closer to his dreams!

 © Shell Education

Name: ______________________________ Date: ______________

Directions: Read "Cooking Competition." Then, answer the questions.

1. What is one challenge in preparing for the cooking competition?
   - (A) Kevin's recipe is too simple.
   - (B) Kevin keeps making some mistakes.
   - (C) Chefs cannot make whatever they like.
   - (D) Adults assist in the kitchen with their kids.

2. Why might Kevin's recipe receive such high praise?
   - (A) He uses quality ingredients.
   - (B) The judges are big fans of pizza.
   - (C) The recipe use just a few ingredients.
   - (D) He uses a sauce that does not need to be cooked.

3. What is Kevin's *craft*?
   - (A) cooking
   - (B) painting
   - (C) sculpting
   - (D) writing

4. What is an antonym for *complicated*?
   - (A) confusing
   - (B) difficult
   - (C) messy
   - (D) simple

5. List three events that support the lesson or theme.

Lesson/Theme: Overcoming challenges can lead to satisfying outcomes.
1.
2.
3.

© Shell Education

Name: ______________________________ Date: ______________

Directions: Reread "Cooking Competition." Then, respond to the prompt.

Pretend you are a judge at the cooking competition. Write to explain criteria you would be looking for to choose a winning dish. Then, describe a favorite food of yours that meets these criteria.

© Shell Education

DAILY TIMES

Kevin's Pizzeria Review

Kevin's Pizzeria is the newest restaurant in town. It's also the tastiest restaurant in town. The menu options allowed me to customize my pizza as much as I wanted. Even the picky eaters in my family were able to find something they liked.

The star of the show at Kevin's is the stone oven style pizza. These pizzas are baked in large stone ovens. The base of each pizza is a thick, crisp dough that will make your mouth water. It's handcrafted and made fresh each morning. Apparently, the dough recipe is a family favorite. It was passed down from Kevin's great grandmother. Layered on the crust is a fresh sauce made of perfectly roasted tomatoes. And on top of the sauce is a layer of fresh mozzarella cheese. You can add various toppings of your choice.

For my meal, I sampled three separate options in stone oven style: classic cheese, pepperoni, and veggie special. Each pizza was delightful. Each one had the perfect amount of toasted cheese, sauce, and toppings. It made for an incredible pizza experience.

Kevin makes sure that only the best ingredients are used in his pizzas. That's why most of the vegetables are grown in his own garden. For the cheese, he works with a local dairy farm. Because they are local, he is able to get it delivered fresh three times a week.

The pizzeria is also dedicated to reducing food waste. Any food left over at the end of the night is given out for free to anyone that needs or wants it.

I highly recommend trying Kevin's Pizzeria if you're on the lookout for new and exciting versions of a classic dish. Your taste buds will not be disappointed!

Name: ______________________ Date: ____________

Directions: Read "Kevin's Pizzeria Review." Then, answer the questions.

1. What does the author mean when they write that the dough is *handcrafted*?
   - (A) made with many hands
   - (B) made carefully by hand
   - (C) made to look like a craft project
   - (D) made following a special recipe

2. Where do most of the ingredients come from?
   - (A) the store
   - (B) the garden
   - (C) a dairy farm
   - (D) a farmer's market

3. What does *on the lookout* mean?
   - (A) to see things clearly
   - (B) to keep a careful eye on
   - (C) to search for something
   - (D) to look from a tall height

4. How does the author feel about the food at Kevin's Pizzeria?
   - (A) It is just okay.
   - (B) It is not worth your time.
   - (C) It is definitely worth trying.
   - (D) It is good, but could be better.

5. Explain how the author's descriptions of the food helped you answer Question 4.

____

____

____

____

____

____

____

____

____

____

____

© Shell Education

Name: ______________________________ Date: ______________

Directions: Closely read these texts. Then, reread the review on page 77. Write your own pizza recipe. Include your favorite ingredients.

Close-Reading Texts

We Love Pizza!	Cooking Competition
Australians also love pizza. If you go to Australia, you can get a pizza with pepperoni. But you can also get a pizza with lamb or eggs on it. Just like in the United States, you can get a pizza with ham and pineapple. Pineapple is the most popular pizza topping in Australia. Some Australians also like cut-up pumpkin on their pizza. Other Australians like shrimp on their pizza.	Measuring out the ingredients for the sauce was the most complicated part. It involved using a variety of fresh garlic, basil, and crushed tomatoes. He also had to use extra virgin olive oil, some salt and pepper, and oregano. He put everything into a bowl and mixed it well.

Name of Pizza ______________________________

Ingredients for the Crust

____

____

____

Ingredients for the Sauce

____

____

____

Toppings

____

____

____

____

Name: ______________________ Date: ______________

Directions: Closely read these texts. Then, compare how chefs in general compare to Kevin when making pizza.

Close-Reading Texts

How to Make Pizza	Kevin's Pizzeria Review
First, the chef will begin by mixing the ingredients for pizza dough, such as flour, yeast, and water. After the dough is mixed, the chef lets the dough rise. Then, it is rolled flat. Most pizzas are circular, but some pizzas look like squares or rectangles. Then, the chef spreads some sauce on the dough. There are several different kinds of sauce options, such as tomato sauce, garlic sauce, or barbecue sauce. Next, the chef adds the toppings and the cheese.	The base of each pizza is a thick, crisp dough that will make your mouth water. It's handcrafted and made fresh each morning. Apparently, the dough recipe is a family favorite. It was passed down from Kevin's great grandmother. Layered on the crust is a fresh sauce made of perfectly roasted tomatoes. And on top of the sauce is a layer of fresh mozzarella cheese. You can add various toppings of your choice.

	Chefs	Kevin
Dough		
Sauce		
Toppings		

 © Shell Education

Name: ______________________________ Date: ________________

Directions: Think about the texts from this unit. Then, respond to the prompt.

Making pizza seems pretty simple. But anything can go wrong at any moment! Write a story about having a challenging experience making pizza. Use dialogue and descriptive language in your story.

Name: ______________________ Date: ______________

Directions: Think about a favorite food at a restaurant you visit. Or, think about your favorite meal. Write a review of the food. Introduce the topic clearly, state an opinion, and support your opinion with reasons. Link your opinion and reasons using words, phrases, and clauses.

DAILY TIMES

Title: ______________________

© Shell Education

Name: ______________________ Date: ______________

Directions: Read the text, and answer the questions.

As You Read

Circle words that indicate two or more things being compared or contrasted.

The Kalahari Desert: A Special Place

The Kalahari Desert is a very special place. It is located in southern Africa. It spans three countries: Botswana, Namibia, and South Africa. Like other deserts, it has lots of sand, and it can get dry and very hot. But the Kalahari is not just a large, empty desert with sand dunes. Unlike many deserts, the Kalahari gets some rainfall. It also has some woodland areas and some dry grassland areas, too. When the summer rains come, flowers and plants bloom. Water holes fill up with rainwater.

Many different kinds of animals live in the Kalahari. When it is very hot and dry, these animals find ways to stay cool. When it rains, they go to the watering holes to drink.

1. On which continent is the Kalahari Desert?
   - (A) Asia
   - (B) Africa
   - (C) Australia
   - (D) North America

2. How is the Kalahari Desert unlike other deserts?
   - (A) It snows there.
   - (B) It gets little rain.
   - (C) It does not have sand dunes.
   - (D) It has woodlands and grasslands.

3. What is the meaning of *span*?
   - (A) goes across
   - (B) goes under
   - (C) is hot
   - (D) rains

4. Which prepositional phrase tells where animals get water?
   - (A) in southern Africa
   - (B) to the watering holes
   - (C) in the Kalahari
   - (D) across Botswana, Namibia, and South Africa

Name: ______________________________ Date: ________________

Directions: Read the text, and answer the questions.

As You Read

Place an exclamation point near surprising or unusual facts.

The Climate in the Kalahari Desert

The Kalahari Desert can get very hot. Summer is the hottest season there. The Kalahari is in the Southern Hemisphere. So, its seasons are different from the Northern Hemisphere. In the desert, summer lasts from November to March. In the summer, temperatures can rise to over 100 degrees during the day. At night, they go down to around 68 or 70 degrees.

It is not always super hot and dry in the Kalahari Desert. Winter lasts from May to August. In the winter, temperatures during the day are about 77 degrees. But the nights can get very cold. Temperatures can drop to 14 degrees! The Kalahari also gets rain sometimes. The rainy season is between November and April. The rainiest month is usually April. When it rains, dry water holes and shallow lakes fill up. Flowers and plants bloom. Animals come to drink.

1. Which statement is true about summer in the Kalahari Desert?
   - (A) Temperatures can drop to 14 degrees.
   - (B) The rainiest month occurs in summer.
   - (C) It is from May to August.
   - (D) Temperatures can rise above 100 degrees.

2. Which phrase describes *when* water holes fill up?
   - (A) when it rains
   - (B) when it gets hot
   - (C) when it gets cold
   - (D) when the seasons change

3. What happens after water holes fill up?
   - (A) Flowers bloom, and animals come to drink.
   - (B) The temperature drops.
   - (C) Plants wither and die.
   - (D) The temperatures rises above 100 degrees.

4. If the rainiest month is *usually* April, what do you know?
   - (A) It never rains in April.
   - (B) It will rain one time in April.
   - (C) April is always the rainiest month.
   - (D) April is most often the rainiest month.

© Shell Education

Name: ______________________ Date: ______________

Directions: Read the text, and answer the questions.

As You Read

Circle plants and animals that live in the Kalahari Desert.
Underline adaptations they have that allow them to live there.

Kalahari Plants and Animals

Many kinds of animals and plants make their homes in the Kalahari Desert. They have found ways to stay cool and get enough water. One type of animal that lives in this desert is the Kalahari lion. Male Kalahari lions have black manes. These lions hunt other desert animals. Most of the animals that they hunt are small, so they have no trouble finding food. Another animal that lives in this desert is the gemsbok. This is a large antelope with long, thin horns. Gemsboks can go for a long time without drinking water. They get the water they need from the plants they eat. Many types of plants live in the Kalahari, too. One important type is the camelthorn tree. This tree makes nutrients for other plants, and those plants become food for animals. The camelthorn tree also offers shade for animals to rest in.

1. What is a *gemsbok*?
   - (A) a tree
   - (B) a lion
   - (C) a plant
   - (D) a large antelope

2. How does the Kalahari lion compare to other lions?
   - (A) It is larger than other lions.
   - (B) It hunts at night unlike other lions.
   - (C) It eats smaller animals than other lions.
   - (D) It does not have a mane.

3. How are animals able to survive in the Kalahari Desert? ______________________

____

4. Would you like to visit the Kalahari Desert? Explain why or why not.

____

____

Name: ______________________________ Date: ________________

As You Read

Place a *B* beside behavioral adaptations of meerkats.
Place a *P* beside physical adaptations of meerkats.

Marvelous Meerkats

Living in the Kalahari Desert isn't easy, but meerkats do it very well. Meerkats are small, furry mammals about two feet long. They are members of the mongoose family. They have sharp claws that they use to dig burrows and look for their food. Meerkats have long tails that they use to help themselves balance when they stand upright. Meerkats spend a lot of time standing upright so that they can watch for danger.

Meerkats are built for life in the harsh desert. They live in underground tunnels, and their eyes have dark circles around them that act like sunglasses. They have special patches of skin on their bellies that absorb the sunlight, which they use to stay warm during the cold desert nights.

Meerkats are social animals. They live in groups called *mobs* or *gangs*. Meerkat mobs work together to stay alive. For example, meerkats look for food during the day. When they are hunting, some meerkats stand guard to watch for enemies. Hawks and eagles like to eat meerkats, and so do other desert animals. So, meerkats always have to be on the lookout. If there is danger, the guards call out a noisy, barking alert. Then, all the meerkats return to their den.

Meerkat families are tight knit groups. Meerkats raise their young together. Baby meerkats are very tiny when they are born. Their eyes are closed and they are helpless. So the adult meerkats all take turns babysitting. They all work together as a team to take care of the baby meerkats. They teach the babies how to look for food and watch out for enemies. Baby meerkats take about a year to mature into adults.

What do meerkats enjoy eating? They usually eat bugs and small rodents, such as mice. Sometimes they eat small snakes, and they can even eat the poisonous scorpion. Its poison does not make them sick. Meerkats are very well adapted for their desert life!

 © Shell Education

Name: ______________________________ Date: ________________

Directions: Read "Marvelous Meerkats." Then, answer the questions.

1. Why do meerkats need sharp claws?
   - (A) They use their claws to climb trees.
   - (B) They use their claws for swimming.
   - (C) They use their claws to dig burrows.
   - (D) They use their claws to take care of the babies.

2. What is one main idea of this text?
   - (A) Meerkats have long tails.
   - (B) Meerkats are social animals.
   - (C) Meerkats live in underground tunnels.
   - (D) Meerkats look for food during the day.

3. Why might meerkats live in underground tunnels?
   - (A) They are too large to live above ground.
   - (B) They cannot see.
   - (C) Tunnels help them keep warm during the cold desert night.
   - (D) They do not like sunlight.

4. How does this text compare to "Kalahari Plants and Animals"?
   - (A) Both texts describe plant adaptations.
   - (B) Both texts describe animal adaptations.
   - (C) Both texts explain how the weather affects animals there.
   - (D) Both texts share opinions as to why life in there is difficult.

5. List details from the text to support the main idea.

Meerkats are well adapted to live in the Kalahari Desert.
1.
2.
3.

Name: ______________________ Date: ______________

Directions: Reread "Marvelous Meerkats." Then, respond to the prompt.

Pretend you are a meerkat. What is your day like? Describe your day in detail.

 © Shell Education

Name: ______________________________ Date: ______________

Directions: Read the text, and answer the questions.

As You Read

Circle words and phrases that describe Miles and his mob.

When I Grow Up

Miles may have only been a meerkat pup, but he knew one thing for certain: family was the most important thing in life. He loved his family. They took care of him, taught him life skills, and made sure he was safe. They even played games with him. He always looked up to his older family members, especially his brother. He also looked up to the elders of other meerkat families, at least those in their mob. He and his mob stuck together through thick or thin because they knew they were stronger in numbers. They could solve problems more easily, finish chores faster, and protect each other more efficiently.

1. What does Miles's family do to show they cared for him?
   - (A) They talk to him.
   - (B) They pay attention to him.
   - (C) They do his chores for him.
   - (D) They help him solve problems.

2. How are Miles and his mob *stronger in numbers*?
   - (A) They work together to be more productive.
   - (B) They are able to better respect their elders.
   - (C) They share ideas among different families.
   - (D) They can play games with large groups.

3. Which idiom may be used to describe Miles's meerkat mob?
   - (A) all ears
   - (B) mad as a hatter
   - (C) thick as thieves
   - (D) water under the bridge

4. What is something that can and should be done *efficiently*?
   - (A) watching a movie
   - (B) eating a picnic lunch
   - (C) raking leaves
   - (D) taking a morning stroll

© Shell Education

Name: ______________________ Date: ____________

Directions: Read the text, and answer the questions.

As You Read

Underline words and phrases that describe the relationship between young and elder meerkats.

Miles and Mort

The oldest meerkats in the mob loved teaching the young meerkats about survival. The young meerkats soaked up all the information they could. Sometimes, young meerkats got survival guidance and lessons from multiple elders. But sometimes, they would only trust one elder.

Miles was one of those meerkats who chose just one—his brother, Mort. Miles had looked up to Mort since he could remember.

Mort was only about a year older than Miles, or about two litters ahead of him, but the two of them had a special bond. Their bond was forged and strengthened when Miles was less than two weeks old. Mort had risked his life to save his younger brother from a hawk. Miles trusted Mort completely and was more than willing to accept Mort's wisdom about survival.

1. Why is the bond so strong between Miles and Mort?
   - (A) They like the same games.
   - (B) They share a common, intense experience.
   - (C) They are the ideal number of litters apart.
   - (D) They team up to learn new things together.

2. What strengthens the bond between Miles and Mort more?
   - (A) empathy
   - (B) enthusiasm
   - (C) trust
   - (D) wisdom

3. What is another word for *forged*?
   - (A) built
   - (B) frolicked
   - (C) promised
   - (D) vented

4. Which word best completes this simile to describe young meerkats? Young meerkats are like _____.
   - (A) cups
   - (B) rain
   - (C) flowers
   - (D) sponges

 © Shell Education

Name: ______________________________ Date: ______________

Directions: Read the text, and answer the questions.

As You Read

Make notes of any connections you can make to the text.

A Lovely Meerkat Morning

Miles and a few of his siblings started their day by sunbathing on a hill. It was the most relaxing morning any meerkat could ask for! Miles decided to stand on his back legs so he could have a look around. He turned toward the high grass. He pointed toward the grass and asked Mort, "What's over there?"

"Over there is food, water, and perhaps a place to catch some shade," Mort said, "but there are also snakes, large animals, and other predators. We only go over there if we are running low on food or water, which reminds me—we actually need to go over there tomorrow."

"What? Are you serious?" Miles asked, starting to panic at the thought of running into a snake.

"I just found out earlier," Mort said, yawning in the sunlight, "The entire mob will head over there tomorrow. You can come, but you must stick by my side and follow my lead because it can be dangerous."

1. What is different about the tall grass?
   - (A) It is far away.
   - (B) It can provide shade.
   - (C) It has survival needs and dangers.
   - (D) It has food, but no water.

2. How does Miles feel about going to the tall grass tomorrow?
   - (A) excited
   - (B) indifferent
   - (C) nervous
   - (D) sad

3. What is dangerous about the tall grass? ______________________________

____

4. Do you think Miles will stick by Mort's side tomorrow? Explain your thinking.

____

____

Name: ______________________________ Date: ________________

As You Read

Make note of any connections you can make to the text.

Hidden Danger

Early the next morning, all the meerkats in the mob began preparing for their journey to the tall grass. Before setting out, the leader came to the front of the mob and made a small speech. He emphasized the importance of having a buddy. Then, he asked them what to do if anything happened.

"Find the nearest escape hole, scatter, and bark to let others know," every meerkat replied in unison.

Miles felt safe beside his brother, but he didn't quite know what to expect.

Mort entered the tall grass, and Miles followed right after him. Mort was finding all types of protein-rich insects when he noticed that Miles had wandered off. Mort quickly scolded Miles for going astray, but Miles couldn't resist the urge to keep exploring.

He was about to pick some delicious berries when he stepped on something round. Eggs! he realized. *What a delicious treat!*

Miles whistled softly and waved Mort over. Scowling, Mort came over to see what Miles had gotten into this time. But his scowl quickly turned to an expression of fear, and something was starting to shake the tall grass.

Confused, Miles darted away from the eggs. He was really glad he had, because a cobra was slithering through the grass beside him! *Those were the cobra's eggs!* Miles suddenly realized.

Quick as lightning, Miles made a beeline for the holes the mob had dug just outside the tall grass. Sensing the cobra was right on his tail, Miles jumped into the first hole he saw. The earth shook behind him, and Miles gulped as he heard a hissing noise—the snake was relentless!

He jumped out of the hole, dived into the next one, and continued doing this several times, hoping to confuse the snake. He made it out of the last hole just as he was out of breath, and he was met with the rest of the mob.

As Miles turned to look behind him, the cobra reared up. Miles winced, but the mob stood tall and barked thunderously at the snake, stopping it in its tracks. Shocked, the snake slithered quickly away, and the mob rejoiced!

"Promise me you'll never go exploring alone again," Mort told Miles. Miles laughed and hugged his brother.

© Shell Education

Name: ______________________ Date: ____________

Directions: Read "Hidden Danger." Then, answer the questions.

1. How do you know the mob is well-practiced?
   - (A) They all follow the leader into the grass.
   - (B) They all recite in unison how to escape danger.
   - (C) Every meerkat has a partner.
   - (D) Every meerkat knows exactly where to find food and water.

2. What is the lesson of the story?
   - (A) Listen to your elders.
   - (B) Don't pick berries.
   - (C) Be careful around meerkats.
   - (D) Do a job right the first time.

3. What does the author mean by Miles is *quick as lightning*?
   - (A) He runs really fast.
   - (B) He is loud like thunder.
   - (C) Lightning strikes beside him.
   - (D) He jumps when he sees a flash of light.

4. What does the author mean by the snake is *right on his tail*?
   - (A) It has a tail like Miles.
   - (B) It catches Miles's tail.
   - (C) It no longer knows where Miles was.
   - (D) It is following close behind him.

5. Write an effect for each cause.

Cause	Effect
The meerkats had dug up a few holes close to the grass line.	
Miles found some eggs.	
All the meerkats barked at the snake.	

Name: ______________________ Date: ______________

Directions: Reread "Hidden Danger." Then, respond to the prompt.

Rewrite the story from the point of view of the snake. Use a variety of transitional words, phrases, and clauses to show the sequence of events.

 © Shell Education

Name: ______________________ Date: ______________

Meerkat Zoo Panel

Meerkat

Suricata suricatta

Found in southern Africa, the meerkat is a highly social mammal of the mongoose family. They can be identified by their gray and brown fur. They have dark circles around their eyes and a dark tip on their tail. They often stand upright. They have pointed snouts and sharp claws to help them dig. They dig to find food and create burrows that they can live in. Meerkats often live in packs of up to 30–40 individuals. The large groups they live in are called mobs. The meerkats in a mob work together to hunt, watch for predators, and raise offspring.

Size: 9.8–13.7 inches (25–35 centimeters) excluding tail

Weight: 1.4–2.1 pounds (0.64–0.95 kilograms)

Diet: mostly insects but sometimes larger prey, such as lizards

Habitat: deserts

Lifespan: up to 8 years in the wild and 12–14 years in captivity

Predators: birds of prey and snakes

Fun fact: Meerkats like to sleep in big piles atop one another!

Meerkat Area

Name: ______________________ Date: ______________

Directions: Read "Meerkat Zoo Panel." Then, answer the questions.

1. How does the map support the text?
   - (A) It shows the color of meerkats in Africa.
   - (B) It shows animals meerkats prey on in Africa.
   - (C) It shows where meerkats may be found in Africa.
   - (D) It shows how meerkats are social animals in Africa.

2. Which detail supports the idea that meerkats are social animals?
   - (A) They live in the desert.
   - (B) They eat mostly insects.
   - (C) They are gray and brown.
   - (D) They hunt and live in mobs.

3. What is another word for *snout*?
   - (A) ear
   - (B) eye
   - (C) mouth
   - (D) nose

4. How do sharp claws help meerkats survive?
   - (A) They use sharp claws to form mobs.
   - (B) They use sharp claws to fend off predators.
   - (C) They use sharp claws to dig shelter and find food.
   - (D) They use sharp claws to help them stand upright.

5. What do you find most interesting about meerkats? Explain your answer.

____

____

____

© Shell Education

Name: ______________________________ Date: ______________

Directions: Closely read these texts. Then, reread the zoo panel on page 95. Write ways meerkats are adapted to live in the desert. Include physical traits and behaviors.

Close-Reading Texts

Marvelous Meerkats	Miles and Mort
Meerkats are built for life in the harsh desert. They live in underground tunnels, and their eyes have dark circles around them that act like sunglasses. They have special patches of skin on their bellies that absorb the sunlight, which they use to stay warm during the cold desert nights.	The oldest meerkats in the mob loved teaching the young meerkats about survival. The young meerkats soaked up all the information they could. Sometimes, young meerkats got survival guidance and lessons from multiple elders. But sometimes, they would only trust one elder.

Ways Meerkats Are Adapted to Live in the Desert

Physical Traits	
Behaviors	

Name: ______________________________ Date: ________________

Directions: Closely read these texts. Describe each animal. Explain what all three animals have in common on the right.

Close-Reading Texts

Kalahari Plants and Animals	Marvelous Meerkats
One type of animal that lives in this desert is the Kalahari lion. Male Kalahari lions have black manes. These lions hunt other desert animals for their meals. Most of the animals that they hunt are small, so they have no trouble finding food. Another animal that lives in this desert is the gemsbok. This is a large antelope with long, thin horns. Gemsboks can go for a long time without drinking water. They get the water they need from the plants they eat.	Meerkats are small, furry mammals about two feet long. They are members of the mongoose family. They have sharp claws that they use to dig burrows and look for their food. Meerkats have long tails that they use to help themselves balance when they stand upright. Meerkats spend a lot of time standing upright so that they can watch for danger.

Animal	Description	What They Have In Common
lion		
gemsbok		
meerkat		

 © Shell Education

Name: ______________________________ Date: ______________

Directions: Reread the texts about meerkats. Then, respond to the prompt.

A documentary is a show or movie that explains facts and details about a topic. Plan a documentary about meerkats. Describe the scenes you will film. Write a narration, or description, for each scene.

Scene	Video	Narration
1		
2		
3		
4		

© Shell Education

Name: ______________________________ Date: ________________

Directions: Find out about other animals that live in the Kalahari Desert. Write a zoo panel for one of the animals.

Zoo Panel

Animal Name: ______________________

____

____

____

____

____

____

____

Size: ______________________

Weight: ______________________

Diet: ______________________

Habitat: ______________________

Lifespan: ______________________

____

____

Predators: ______________________

____

Fun fact: ______________________

____

____

____

____

© Shell Education

Name: ______________________________ Date: ______________

Directions: Read the text, and answer the questions.

As You Read

Circle words that indicate comparisons. Underline what is being compared.

Habitable Planets

Earth can support a variety of life because of where it is in the solar system. Earth doesn't get too much or too little of the sun's heat. This spot in the solar system is known as the *habitable zone*. So, plants, animals, and people can all thrive on the planet.

There are seven other planets in the solar system. But only two others lie in the habitable zone. They are Venus and Mars. Yet these planets lack some of the life-supporting factors that Earth has. For example, the atmosphere on Mars is too thin to allow for liquid water to stay on the surface of the planet. The atmosphere on Venus is too thick and does not have enough oxygen.

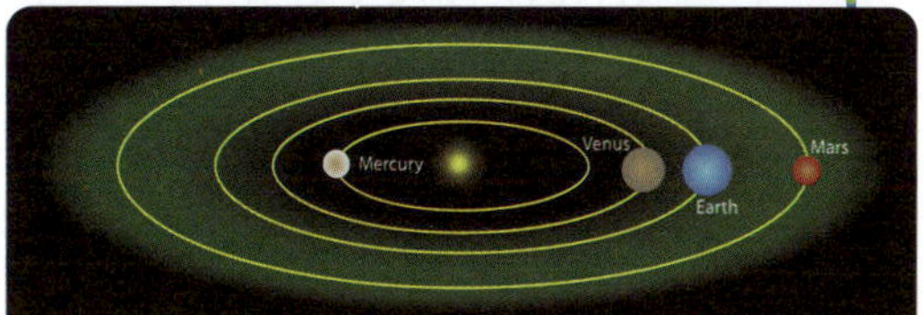

Solar System

1. What is the main idea of this text?
   - (A) Earth is one of eight planets.
   - (B) Earth is in the right spot in the solar system to support life.
   - (C) The atmosphere on Mars is too thin.
   - (D) Three planets are in the habitable zone with Earth.

2. Why can Venus and Mars not support life?
   - (A) They are too hot.
   - (B) They are not in the habitable zone.
   - (C) Their atmospheres are not suitable.
   - (D) They are too far away from the sun.

3. How is *yet* used in the text?
   - (A) as an adverb to describe time
   - (B) as a conjunction to show contrast
   - (C) as a noun to show something is unclear
   - (D) as an adjective to describe the habitable zone

4. What is another word for *habitable*?
   - (A) liquid
   - (B) greatest
   - (C) centered
   - (D) livable

© Shell Education

Name: ______________________________ Date: ______________

Directions: Read the text, and answer the questions.

As You Read

Underline new or interesting words related to space.

Earth and Its Cosmic Address

Earth has a precise location in the universe. It is somewhat similar to how you have an address at your home. Some scientists refer to Earth's location as its cosmic address. This address tells people where Earth is located.

Earth orbits a star in a solar system. This solar system sits inside the Milky Way Galaxy. A galaxy is a very large group of stars, planets, and other matter. Outside the Milky Way is a group of about 30 other galaxies. Together, these galaxies make up a local group. And even more galaxies are outside this group. Combined, they make up a local supercluster. A supercluster is another word for a massive group of galaxies. And outside of that are even more superclusters. All these groups of stars and planets exist in the universe.

To get a planet's cosmic address, you would start with the name of the planet, the solar system, and the galaxy. Then, you would add the name of the local group and the local supercluster. You would end with the universe!

1. How are planets in distant galaxies related to Earth?
   - (A) They are inside the universe.
   - (B) They have the same address.
   - (C) They are in the same solar system.
   - (D) They are within the Milky Way Galaxy.

2. What is meant by *cosmic*?
   - (A) far away
   - (B) in the universe
   - (C) at an address
   - (D) linear

3. About how many galaxies make up a local group with the Milky Way?
   - (A) three
   - (B) thirteen
   - (C) thirty
   - (D) three hundred

4. What is the name of Earth's galaxy?
   - (A) Local Group
   - (B) Local Supercluster
   - (C) Milky Way
   - (D) Universe

 © Shell Education

Name: ______________________________ Date: ______________

Directions: Read the text, and answer the questions.

As You Read

Write clarifying questions you have about the text in the margin.

Gravity

The same force that causes a ball to fall to the ground is what causes Earth to continue orbiting the sun. This force is gravity. It is dependent on how much mass an object has. The mass of an object is a measurement of how much weight it has. Objects with more mass have more gravity, and objects with less mass have less gravity.

black hole

Sometimes, objects in space have too much mass. These objects can form black holes. A black hole is a point in space where gravity is so great that not even light can escape. Some black holes are bigger than others. Large black holes are at the center of every galaxy. They are supermassive black holes. The supermassive black hole at the center of the Milky Way is known as Sagittarius A. The mass of this black hole is equal to about four million suns!

1. How is mass related to gravity?
   - (A) Objects with greater mass have less gravity.
   - (B) Objects with greater mass have greater gravity.
   - (C) Objects with less mass have greater gravity.
   - (D) Mass is not related to gravity.

2. Which force keeps Earth in orbit?
   - (A) black hole
   - (B) light
   - (C) mass
   - (D) gravity

3. How does a black hole form? ______________________________

____

4. Do you think scientists will discover more black holes? Explain your thinking.

____

____

© Shell Education

Name: ______________________________ Date: ______________

As You Read

Circle facts about Hubble. Underline facts about the James Webb Space Telescope.

A Brief History of Space Telescopes

Telescopes have come a long way through time. Galileo Galilei was the first person to use a telescope to look at objects in space. He looked at Jupiter's moons. Science has improved a lot since Galilei's time. We even have telescopes set up in outer space! These are known as space telescopes.

Space telescopes are set up in special ways. They are placed far away from any source of light on Earth. This way, they do not have to deal with light from large cities or countries. Astronomers call this light noise. Space telescopes are great because they deal with less noise. This way, the images that they can show are more clear and defined.

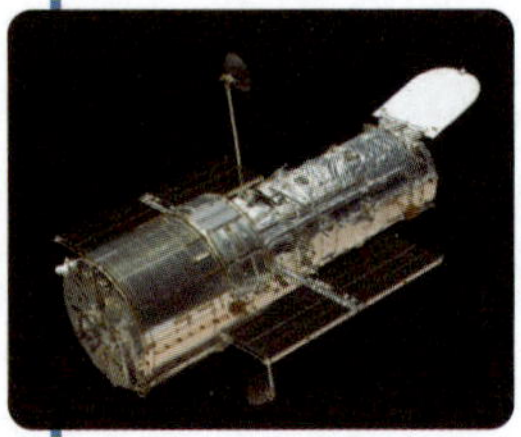

The Hubble Space Telescope (HST) was the fourth space telescope to be put into space. It was the first one that looked at objects in outer space through the visible spectrum. This is a fancy way of saying that it sees things the same way people on Earth see things. The Hubble led to a lot of discoveries.

An even more powerful space telescope was launched. It is the James Webb Space Telescope (JWST). The National Aeronautics and Space Administration (NASA) launched this telescope on December 25, 2021. One of the main differences between the JWST and Hubble is the size of their mirrors. The mirror on a telescope is also called an eye. The mirror on the JWST is almost three times wider than Hubble's. This bigger mirror allows the JWST to see objects that are fainter and farther away.

There are more differences between the two telescopes that make the JWST stronger. The JWST sees light in the infrared range. This is light that is outside the visible spectrum. Anything that gives off heat can be seen in the infrared range. But the Hubble primarily sees things that are in the visible range of light. So, JWST can see things that the Hubble cannot. One example is the atmosphere of a planet. This can be seen in the infrared range. Another difference is that the Hubble has problems seeing through space dust. But space dust is mostly seen in the visible spectrum. Since the JWST uses infrared, it can see what is beyond the dust.

Space telescopes have improved a lot in the past few decades. There are exciting things to see in space in the future!

 © Shell Education

Name: ______________________ Date: ______________

Directions: Read "Hidden Danger." Then, answer the questions.

1. How many space telescopes came before Hubble?
   - Ⓐ one
   - Ⓑ two
   - Ⓒ three
   - Ⓓ four

2. Why are space telescopes beneficial?
   - Ⓐ They have fewer mirrors.
   - Ⓑ They do not send information back quickly.
   - Ⓒ Light does not interfere with them.
   - Ⓓ They deal with more noise.

3. What is a limitation of Hubble?
   - Ⓐ It does not take clear images.
   - Ⓑ It cannot see through space dust.
   - Ⓒ It sees objects in infrared light.
   - Ⓓ It cannot travel as far as others.

4. What does an astronomer do?
   - Ⓐ make space telescopes
   - Ⓑ study zodiac signs
   - Ⓒ travel to space
   - Ⓓ study space

5. Compare Hubble to the James Webb Space Telescope.

Hubble	**James Webb**
Both	

Name: ______________________________ Date: ______________

Directions: Reread "A Brief History of Space Telescopes" and the other texts from this week. Then, respond to the prompt.

What lies in space beyond Earth? Write a topic sentence. Develop the topic with facts, definitions, and concrete details, from one or more texts.

© Shell Education

Name: ____________________ Date: ____________

Directions: Read the text, and answer the questions.

As You Read

Circle words that describe people's feelings.

Star Stuff

Normally, Naomi would be excited to start a new school year. But she had moved to a new town a few weeks before, and she was feeling anxious.

"Whenever you feel nervous, take a deep breath," her dad told her. "Then think about how—"

"You and I are made out of the same stuff stars are made of," Naomi said, finishing her father's favorite phrase. They both loved Carl Sagan, and her father often told her how his work was informative and inspirational.

Naomi hoped she would be able to tell the class what she had done over the summer. For the past few months, Naomi had been going to space camp. She had learned about stars, planets, astronauts, and space technology. She even got to go on a ride that simulated what it felt like to be in space!

Naomi hoped that the rest of the class would be as interested in space as she was.

1. What was Carl Sagan most likely interested in?
   - (A) camps
   - (B) family events
   - (C) school
   - (D) space

2. Why does Naomi's dad begin to say an inspirational quote?
   - (A) She is excited to learn about space.
   - (B) She is nervous about starting school.
   - (C) She is excited about her summer camp.
   - (D) She is nervous about the space simulator.

3. How does Naomi feels about space camp?
   - (A) She loves it.
   - (B) She hates it.
   - (C) She finds it boring.
   - (D) She thinks it is okay.

4. What is the meaning of *simulated*?
   - (A) acted like
   - (B) forbid
   - (C) raced around
   - (D) tried

Name: ______________________________ Date: ______________

Directions: Read the text, and answer the questions.

As You Read

Make notes in the margins about connections you can make to Naomi's first day at school.

Ms. Findelton

Ms. Findelton went to the front of the room and greeted everyone.

"Hello! Welcome! My name is Ms. Findelton. I'd like us to go around the room and introduce ourselves. I'll start by telling you a little bit about myself. I've been teaching for five years, I have two cats, and my favorite subject is science. I'd like everyone to start thinking of their favorite subject in school."

Naomi grinned at her. The entire class began to mumble amongst themselves. Ms. Findelton broke the chatter with a question.

"Okay, let's see...whose favorite subject is science?"

Naomi's hand shot up immediately. Ms. Findelton chuckled.

"Um, Hi, I'm Naomi," Naomi said shyly. "I just moved here. I love learning about the stuff around us. That includes Earth, space, plants, and oceans."

1. What is the class likely mumbling about?
   - (A) going to recess
   - (B) their favorite subjects
   - (C) the classroom decorations
   - (D) the lunch menu

2. What does this sentence from the text tell readers about Naomi?
   Naomi's hand shot up immediately.
   - (A) She is excited to share.
   - (B) She is nervous.
   - (C) She is not sure what to share.
   - (D) She does not want to be called on.

3. Which of the following is the best description of *chatter*?
   - (A) smiling
   - (B) talking
   - (C) whispering
   - (D) yelling

4. Why does Naomi like science?
   - (A) She likes using scientific equipment.
   - (B) She likes experiments.
   - (C) She likes learning about the world.
   - (D) She likes to work with lab partners.

© Shell Education

Name: ______________________ Date: ____________

Directions: Read the text, and answer the questions.

As You Read

Write comments or questions you have about the events in the text.

Let's Talk Science

"Would you like to share anything fun you did over the summer?" Ms. Findelton asked Naomi. Naomi smiled and nodded.

"I went to space camp over the summer," she said. A few of her classmates said *Wow!* or *Ooh!* out loud. "I got to eat some freeze-dried ice cream just like astronauts eat in space, and I even got to see the shuttles at the space center."

Ms. Findelton went around the room so every student could introduce themselves. Naomi was relieved to hear that there were a few other students who also loved space, and she couldn't wait to talk with them at recess.

"Space is actually our first science topic this year. I want you to write everything you know about space on a sheet of notebook paper."

Naomi began writing frantically in her notebook. After a few minutes, Ms. Findelton gave new directions. They were going to watch a short video about the universe. Naomi quickly flipped to a new page in her notebook.

1. What is another way to say *frantically*?
   - (A) with care
   - (B) with caution
   - (C) with disinterest
   - (D) with enthusiasm

2. Who does Naomi hope to talk with at recess?
   - (A) her classmates who don't know much about space
   - (B) her classmates from camp
   - (C) students in a different class
   - (D) her classmates who also love space

3. How do you know Naomi is excited about school? ______________________

____

4. Does space camp sound exciting to you? Why or why not? ______________

____

Name: ______________________________ Date: ______________

As You Read

Underline events that seem unrealistic. Write comments or questions you have about the events in the text.

A Strange Trip to Europa

"This is the surface of Jupiter's icy moon, Europa. The ice on the surface is around 10 to 15 miles or 15 to 25 kilometers thick," the narrator of the video said. Naomi struggled to keep up with the narrator as she took notes furiously. She was starting to feel tired and it didn't help that Ms. Findelton dimmed the lights.

Maybe I can close my eyes for just one moment, Naomi thought to herself. When she opened her eyes again, the classroom had faded. It seemed like she was alone on an ice-covered moon! She saw a large, spinning ball of gas hanging in the blackness of the sky. She had learned a lot about the planets, and it seemed like she was looking at Jupiter. *Am I on Europa?*

"Jupiter is held in orbit by the sun's gravity," a faraway voice echoed.

Naomi spun around, trying to figure out where the voice was coming from. Then, she started to feel vibrations coming from the ground beneath her. The ice beneath her feet was beginning to splinter and form cracks. *An earthquake!* Naomi thought to herself, her heart pounding. She turned to run, but her shoes seemed like they were glued to the ice.

"This part is very important, so please pay attention," another voice echoed.

Naomi looked down at her feet. They were now off the ground—she was floating! Large chunks of ice were floating up around her. When Naomi looked back up into the sky, she saw she was being pulled toward a large black hole.

A sharp *plink* noise woke Naomi up from her dream. She blinked and realized she had fallen asleep. Her pencil had fallen to the floor, and she leaned over in her chair to grab it.

Whew! That was just a dream, Naomi thought to herself, shuddering as she recalled the ice. Then, she looked down at her page of notes. It was only half-filled, and the video was nearly over!

When the video ended, Ms. Findelton turned on the lights and asked everyone to get into groups to share what they had learned. A student sitting a few chairs away from Naomi startled himself awake. Naomi grinned and headed over to him, sure that they would have plenty of things to talk about.

 © Shell Education

Name: ______________________ Date: ______________

Directions: Read "A Strange Trip to Europa." Then, answer the questions.

1. What is Europa?
   - (A) a planet in our solar system
   - (B) one of Jupiter's moons
   - (C) one of Mars' moons
   - (D) a made up planet

2. How does Naomi feel about the vibration underground?
   - (A) excited
   - (B) annoyed
   - (C) frightened
   - (D) indifferent

3. What is an synonym for *shuddering*?
   - (A) breaking
   - (B) floating
   - (C) dancing
   - (D) quivering

4. Why is Naomi concerned when she wakes up?
   - (A) She misses information in the video.
   - (B) She worries her teacher would be angry.
   - (C) She is sure her classmates will laugh at her.
   - (D) She worries that she will not get to sleep that night.

5. Describe different parts of Naomi's dream-space adventure.

Europa	
Jupiter	
earthquake	
gravity	

Name: ______________________ Date: ______________

Directions: Reread "A Strange Trip to Europa." Then, respond to the prompt.

Imagine that you have the chance to go to space for a day. Write a story about your day and the things you see. Orient the reader by introducing the setting, a situation or problem, and a narrator and/or characters. Organize the events to unfold naturally.

© Shell Education

Name: ______________________________ Date: ______________

Naomi's Adventure Comic

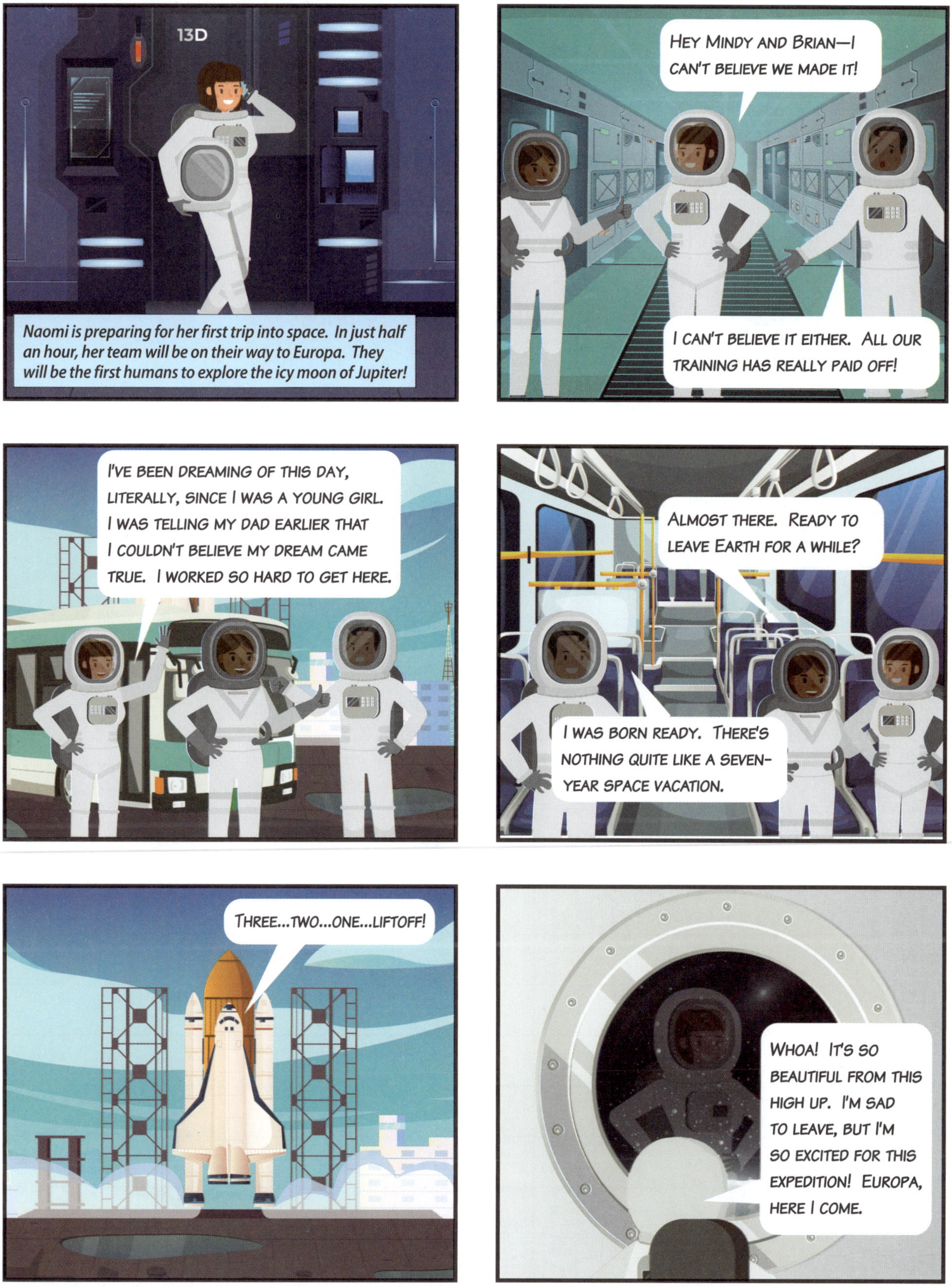

Name: ______________________ Date: ____________

Directions: Read "Naomi's Adventure Comic." Then, answer the questions.

1. Why is Naomi's space mission important?
   - (A) It's the first mission beyond Mars.
   - (B) It's the first mission where people explore space.
   - (C) It's the first time people will encounter aliens.
   - (D) It's the first time people will go to Jupiter's moon.

2. Why do you think they are going to be gone for seven years?
   - (A) They think that seven is a lucky number.
   - (B) It takes a long time to go anywhere in space.
   - (C) They will go around Europa seven times.
   - (D) All missions to space take exactly seven years.

3. How does Naomi feel about leaving Earth?
   - (A) scared and annoyed
   - (B) sad but excited
   - (C) confused and sad
   - (D) nervous but disappointed

4. What is another word for an *expedition*?
   - (A) journey
   - (B) travel bags
   - (C) travel group
   - (D) vehicle

5. What do you envision Naomi and her crew will do on their way to Europa? What do you think they will do when they arrive?

____

____

____

____

____

____

____

 © Shell Education

Name: ______________________________ Date: ______________

Directions: Closely read these texts. Then, reread the comic on page 113. Write an interjection from each passage. Explain why the author used it.

Close-Reading Texts

Let's Talk Science	A Strange Trip to Europa
"I went to space camp over the summer," she said. A few of her classmates said *Wow!* or *Ooh!* out loud. "I got to eat some freeze-dried ice cream just like astronauts eat in space, and I even got to see the shuttles at the space center."	*Whew! That was just a dream,* Naomi thought to herself, shuddering as she recalled the ice. Then she looked down at her page of notes. It was only half-filled, and the video was nearly over!

Text	Interjection	Purpose or Meaning
Let's Talk Science		
A Strange Trip to Europa		
Naomi's Adventure Comic		

Name: ______________________________ Date: ______________

Directions: Closely read these texts. Then, reread the comic on page 113. Record Naomi's feelings. Describe her actions or story events that reveal her feelings.

Close-Reading Texts

Star Stuff	Let's Talk Science
Normally, Naomi would be excited to start a new school year. But she had moved to a new town a few weeks before, and she was feeling anxious. "Whenever you feel nervous, take a deep breath," her dad told her. "Then think about how—" "You and I are made out of the same stuff stars are made of," Naomi said, finishing her father's favorite phrase.	Naomi was relieved to hear that there were a few other students who also loved space, and she couldn't wait to talk with them at recess. "Space is actually our first science topic this year is. I want you to write everything you know—or think you know—about space on a sheet of notebook paper." Naomi began writing frantically in her notebook.

Text	Naomi's Feelings	Story Support
Star Stuff		
Let's Talk Science		
Naomi's Adventure Comic		

 © Shell Education

Name: ______________________ Date: ______________

Directions: Reread the texts in this unit. Then, respond to the prompt.

Explain why you would or would not want to be an astronaut when you grow up. Link your opinion and reasons using words, phrases, and clauses.

© Shell Education

Name: ______________________________ Date: ________________

Directions: Galactic Travel Tours has a special on a space flight. Make a comic in which you join a flight. Describe where you go and what you see and do. Use speech bubbles to show dialogue.

 © Shell Education

Name: ______________________________ Date: ________________

Directions: Read the text, and answer the questions.

As You Read

Circle things you would like to do if you visited Auckland.

Auckland, New Zealand

Imagine a place where you can swim, take a boat or ferry ride, and visit a park all in the same city. If you visit Auckland, New Zealand, you can do all these things! Auckland is the biggest city in New Zealand. Auckland is sometimes called "the city of sails." That is because it is famous for its sailing and yacht races. Auckland is also home to Sky Tower. Sky Tower is the tallest building in the Southern Hemisphere. People can go to the top of Sky Tower and see for miles around. More fun things to do around the city include going on dolphin or whale-watching tours, visiting the zoo, or following the many bike paths. Plus, there are countless stores and restaurants. So no matter what you like to do, you can find something fun to do in Auckland!

1. Why is Auckland sometimes called "the city of sails"?
   - (A) It is home to Sky Tower.
   - (B) It is the largest city in New Zealand.
   - (C) It is famous for sailing and yacht racing.
   - (D) You can go dolphin and whale watching.

2. What is a *yacht*?
   - (A) food
   - (B) a boat
   - (C) an animal
   - (D) a shoe

3. How can you tell the author wants the reader to be excited about Auckland?
   - (A) They use exclamations.
   - (B) They describe important sites.
   - (C) They explain why Auckland is famous.
   - (D) They describe their favorite thing to do.

4. What is the main idea of this text?
   - (A) Auckland is on New Zealand's North Island.
   - (B) Everyone should avoid Auckland, New Zealand.
   - (C) There fun things to do in Auckland, New Zealand.
   - (D) The tallest building in the Southern Hemisphere is in Auckland.

© Shell Education

Name: ______________________ Date: ______________

Directions: Read the text, and answer the questions.

As You Read

Underline facts you learn about rugby.

A National Sport

Can you guess which sport this is from the following clues? This sport is played in over 100 countries. It is played with fifteen players on each team. The object of the game is to carry the ball over the opponents' goal line. Have you guessed the sport yet? It's rugby!

Rugby is extremely popular in many countries of the world. It is the national sport of New Zealand, South Africa, Wales, and other countries. Rugby is getting more popular, and it was even included in the 2016 Olympics.

Rugby is like American football in some ways. For example, in both rugby and American football, the ball has an oval shape. Players try to carry it down the field. But there are some key differences between the two sports. In each sport, there are different rules for how the ball can be moved.

1. What is one main idea of this text?
   - (A) Rugby is played with 15 players on each team.
   - (B) Rugby is played in over 100 countries.
   - (C) Rugby is popular in many countries.
   - (D) Rugby has a ball with an oval shape.

2. Which prepositional phrase explains where rugby is played?
   - (A) in over 100 countries
   - (B) down field
   - (C) over the opponents' goal line
   - (D) with fifteen players

3. What are opponents?
   - (A) players on the other team
   - (B) players on the same team
   - (C) the national sport of New Zealand
   - (D) popular countries around the world

4. Which word reflects how the author describes rugby?
   - (A) limited
   - (B) safe
   - (C) popular
   - (D) varied

© Shell Education

Name: ______________________________ Date: ______________

Directions: Read the text, and answer the questions.

As You Read

Circle words that describe the Māori.

The Māori

The Māori (MAU-ree) are Indigenous (in-DIH-juh-nuhs) people of New Zealand. That means they were the first people to live there. The Māori are Polynesian like the Indigenous peoples of Hawai'i. Nobody knows when Māori people first came to New Zealand. But it is known how they got there. They came to New Zealand in canoes. They came from other parts of the Pacific. The Māori were very skilled sailors.

Today, about 14 percent of New Zealand's people are Māori. The Māori people have their own culture. They have their own language, customs, and legends. They have a strong sense of community, too. Māori songs and art are famous. Their tattoos are famous as well.

1. According to the text, what are the Māori skilled at doing?
   - (A) amusement parks
   - (B) cooking
   - (C) fishing
   - (D) sailing

2. The word *percent* means *for each one hundred*. Which word has a Latin root with a similar meaning?
   - (A) center
   - (B) century
   - (C) perfect
   - (D) person

3. What is still uncertain about the Māori? ______________________________

____

____

4. What image would you add to this text to give readers more information?

____

____

© Shell Education

Name: ______________________________ Date: ______________

As You Read

Underline information that is new or interesting.

Kia Ora! Welcome to New Zealand

Kia ora (kee OR-uh)! This is something you may hear if you visit the island country of New Zealand. *Kia ora* means *hello* in the Māori language. Māori is one language spoken in New Zealand. English is also spoken there. There is a lot more to learn about New Zealand!

First, New Zealand's geography is unique. The country is located in the Pacific Ocean. New Zealand has two main islands: North Island and South Island. Together, they are about the size of the U.S. state of Colorado. The capital of New Zealand is Wellington. Wellington is on the North Island. So is Auckland, which is the country's largest city. But most of New Zealand is not made up of very large cities. Instead, there are many smaller cities and towns.

New Zealand is in the Southern Hemisphere, so the seasons there are different from the seasons in the Northern Hemisphere. For example, when it is winter in the United States, it is summer in New Zealand. The North Island is usually a little warmer than the South Island.

Although New Zealand is not a large country, there are many things for people to see and do there. On the South Island, there are beautiful mountains where people can ski and snowboard. There are several beaches, forests, and lakes to visit. On the North Island, people can see volcanoes and hot springs. They can visit New Zealand's two largest cities, too.

Lots of animals thrive in New Zealand. Many types of fish, whales, and dolphins live in the surrounding waters. Different types of birds live across the land. The most famous bird is the kiwi. It is a flightless bird about the size of a chicken. New Zealanders are sometimes even called Kiwis.

A few sports are popular in New Zealand. The national sport of New Zealand is rugby. It is the most popular sport in the country. Rugby is similar in some ways to American football. Other popular sports in New Zealand include sailing and cricket. Cricket is similar in some ways to American baseball. Many people throughout the country play or watch these sports.

Whether you visit the North or South Island of New Zealand, there is plenty for you to see and do. With many places to visit, sports to see, and weather to enjoy, New Zealand has countless options!

 © Shell Education

Name: ______________________ Date: ______________

Directions: Read "*Kia Ora*! Welcome to New Zealand." Then, answer the questions.

1. What are New Zealanders sometimes called?
   - (A) Crickets
   - (B) Islanders
   - (C) Kia Ora
   - (D) Kiwis

2. What is one main idea of this text?
   - (A) *Kia ora* means *hello* in Māori.
   - (B) Cricket is a game a little like baseball.
   - (C) The capital of New Zealand is Wellington.
   - (D) New Zealand is an island country in the Pacific Ocean.

3. What is main idea of fifth paragraph?
   - (A) Auckland is the largest city in New Zealand.
   - (B) People in New Zealand play cricket and rugby.
   - (C) New Zealand is home to many types of animals.
   - (D) A kiwi is a flightless bird about the size of a chicken.

4. What do you learn about in this text and in "The Māori"?
   - (A) The Māori are sailors.
   - (B) The Māori children go to school.
   - (C) The Māori have their own language.
   - (D) The Māori came to New Zealand in canoes.

5. List details about each topic as it relates to New Zealand.

Topic	Details
South Island	
North Island	
Animals	
Sports	

Name: ____________________ Date: ____________

Directions: Reread "*Kia Ora*! Welcome to New Zealand" and the other texts from this week. Then, respond to the prompt.

How does life in New Zealand compare to where you live? Write a paragraph about the similarities and differences between life in New Zealand and your home.

 © Shell Education

Name: ______________________________ Date: ______________

Directions: Read the text, and answer the questions.

As You Read

Circle reasons for the welcoming event. Underline things that take place.

Preparing for the Festival

It was an exciting week for Kaia and her family. They were volunteering for the annual summer festival at their local community center in Auckland. Kaia's family was Māori, and they often volunteered for this event. It was a weekend filled with special introductions, music, dancing, and feasts. During this time, people in her community met with tourists from around the world, talked about their cultures, and had a good time.

This year, the event was extra special for Kaia. Her family would be bringing a guest: Kaia's pen pal, Jacob. Jacob lived in Montreal, Canada, and he had always wanted to visit New Zealand. Kaia couldn't wait for him to arrive in a couple of days!

Her family would go to the community center later to put up decorations, but for right now, she was helping her mom with some cooking. Kaia spent her day running around the kitchen, chopping vegetables, and preparing ingredients. She hoped Jacob would enjoy the meals they were making!

1. Why does Kaia's family help with the annual summer festival?
   - (A) to meet new people and share their culture
   - (B) to greet guests as official New Zealand greeters
   - (C) to offer entertainment for visiting government officials
   - (D) to show Jacob's family why New Zealand was so popular

2. What is another word for *annual*?
   - (A) daily
   - (B) weekly
   - (C) monthly
   - (D) yearly

3. How does Kaia spend her time in this story?
   - (A) cleaning
   - (B) cooking
   - (C) setting up banners
   - (D) stocking supplies

4. Which phrase best describes where Jacob lives?
   - (A) He is from Montreal.
   - (B) He is from Auckland.
   - (C) He is from New Zealand.
   - (D) He is from Seattle.

Name: ______________________________ Date: ________________

Directions: Read the text, and answer the questions.

As You Read

Write questions or comments you have about the events and characters in margins.

Arriving in Auckland

A few days later, Jacob arrived! Kaia was nervous to meet him, but within five minutes of meeting, they were joking and laughing. Kaia showed Jacob around her neighborhood, and he loved the fried whitebait fish they had for dinner.

The next day, Kaia brought Jacob to the community center. They walked up behind one of her elders, and she tapped his shoulder.

"Hey Koa, this is Jacob," Kaia said. "He's my pen pal from Montreal."

Koa turned and smiled. "Glad to meet you, Jacob," he said. "Have you been enjoying Auckland so far?"

"It's been great," Jacob said. "Everything is so new to me!"

Koa smiled at Jacob, "I'm sure you'll love the festival. We'll be having music, introductions from other tribes, and, of course, food!"

1. How is Jacob feeling about being in Auckland?
   - (A) He feels excited to be learning new things.
   - (B) He is scared to be there.
   - (C) He is nervous to try new food.
   - (D) He feels unsure about meeting Kaia.

2. What words best describe Koa?
   - (A) timid but welcoming
   - (B) friendly but harsh
   - (C) formal and nice
   - (D) welcoming and friendly

3. What prefix can be added to *arranging* to create a new word?
   - (A) *in–*
   - (B) *dis–*
   - (C) *re–*
   - (D) *un–*

4. Which word is **not** a compound word?
   - (A) handshake
   - (B) whitebait
   - (C) neighborhood
   - (D) welcoming

 © Shell Education

Name: ______________________________ Date: ________________

Directions: Read the text, and answer the questions.

As You Read

Write questions or comments you have about the events and characters in margins.

Learning about Legends

The first day of the festival had arrived. Kaia and Jacob were handing out programs when Jacob overheard a conversation between two friends.

"No, no, no, earth mother and sky father were pushed apart by all their children except for the god of wind and storms," one of the friends said.

"Oh, that's right! And *then* the god of wind and storms raged war against his siblings," the other friend said. "He went on to beat them all, *except* for one brother—the god of people."

"I think they were talking about a Māori legend," Jacob said to Kaia. "In school, we learned about some First Nations legends, but I had not heard any Māori legends before. Can you tell me about any others?"

"Hmm…well, my favorite legend is of the whale rider. It's a long story, but basically, this guy rode a whale from one island to another!"

1. What are the two friends talking about?
   - (A) a type of Māori artwork
   - (B) a Māori legend
   - (C) a Māori tradition
   - (D) a Māori symbol

2. Why are the words *except* and *then* italicized in the text?
   - (A) to show they are part of the dialogue
   - (B) to show they are vocabulary words
   - (C) to give them more emphasis
   - (D) to give them a special accent

3. What is Kaia's favorite legend about? ______________________________

____

4. How do you think stories and legends contribute to a culture? ______________

____

Name: ______________________________ Date: ____________________

As You Read

Underline details about Kaia's culture. Put a star next to details about Jacob's culture.

Having Fun at the Festival

Kaia and Jacob went inside and found their seats. Koa went to the stage and began speaking into a microphone.

"*Kia ora!* Welcome to the first day of our annual festival!" Koa said to a thunderous round of applause from the crowd. "I'll keep this short and sweet since I know everyone can smell the seafood our volunteers are grilling outside."

Kaia nudged Jacob and whispered to him, "I seriously cannot wait."

"I always love this time of year," Koa said. "I've talked to so many wonderful people from around the world, even some as far away as Canada."

Jacob's mouth fell open in surprise as Koa smiled at him from the stage.

"I'd just like to say thanks to all of you for being here," Koa continued, "and I hope you have a wonderful time over the next few days. I know that there's so much we can all learn from each other."

When Koa finished speaking, they headed straight for the seafood buffet outside. Jacob filled his paper plate to the brim with a variety of fried fish, mussels, and some lobster. Kaia led Jacob to a table where one of her friends was sitting.

"Hey Manu!" Kaia said. "This is Jacob, my pen pal from Canada."

Manu's eyes went wide. Jacob almost thought he had started choking on the bit of fish he was eating, but then Manu launched into a bunch of questions.

"Canada, no way, are you serious?" Manu asked. "I have always wanted to go to Canada. Do you speak any French? Maybe we could practice together if you do. Is it true that it's winter over there right now? And do you like poutine? Oh man, I have always wanted to try poutine."

Kaia laughed and whispered to Jacob, "Manu gets a little excited sometimes, but that's why I love him."

Jacob realized that for all the things he wanted to know and learn about New Zealand, Manu and Kaia wanted to learn the same thing about Canada. After answering Manu's questions, Jacob asked Manu and Kaia more about Māori culture, particularly the legends. By the end of the first day of the festival, he had no idea how he would be able to sleep after all the excitement. He couldn't wait to do it all again tomorrow!

 © Shell Education

Name: ______________________________ Date: ______________

Directions: Read "Having Fun at the Festival." Then, answer the questions.

1. What is the main point of Koa's speech?
   - (A) He hopes everyone tries all the food.
   - (B) He hopes everyone will learn from one another.
   - (C) He hopes people will be nice to on another.
   - (D) He hopes people will ask him questions.

2. How does Jacob feel about Manu's questions?
   - (A) He feels nervous his answers will not be interesting.
   - (B) He feels annoyed by the long list of questions.
   - (C) He feels happy to share things about Canada.
   - (D) He wonders why Manu wants to know so much.

3. What is a antonym for *thunderous*?
   - (A) audible
   - (B) loud
   - (C) quiet
   - (D) shocking

4. What can you infer about how the three friends feel about their day?
   - (A) They are glad it is the last day of the festival.
   - (B) They have fun at the festival but do not like the food.
   - (C) They are tired and overwhelmed.
   - (D) They enjoy learning about each other's cultures.

5. Summarize four events that happen in story in the order they occur.

1.	
2.	
3.	
4.	

Name: ______________________________ Date: ______________

Directions: Reread "Having Fun at the Festival." Then, respond to the prompt.

Imagine that you have a pen pal. Write a letter to your pen pal, telling them about what life is like where you live. Use descriptive words and phrases and sensory details to tell them about your home and life.

 © Shell Education

Name: ______________________ Date: ______________

11:11 100%

KAIA'S BLOG

Hello faithful readers,

Growing up as an Indigenous person in New Zealand meant that I always participated in traditions. My family really strived to stay connected to Māori culture. I used to think that everyone knew about Māori practices. But after volunteering for the annual summer festival in Auckland, I realized there is so much information I can share with people.

That's why I'm here to give a brief overview of my culture! My plan is to make this into a series. I want to focus on a specific theme each week. For today, I really want to dive into artistic traditions. This will include carving, weaving, and physical performances.

First, we'll talk about visual arts. Many Māori patterns in art are inspired by nature. You might see art that features spider webs or fish scales. Or maybe you'll see the delicate curled leaves of a fern tree. These patterns can be found in wood carvings. They can also be found in pounamu stone and bone carvings.

Māori performing arts are called kapa haka. These performances include dancing. These also include chanting and singing. There are many kinds of performances. One type of performance is the haka. The haka is a ceremonial dance performed in a group. It's done this way to signify the unity of the tribe. It also shows strength and pride of the tribe. Another performance is waitata-a-ringa. Performers sing while moving their hands quickly when they perform. They do this to represent water, wind, and heat. An important part of kapa haka is the facial expressions made by the performers. These expressions are called pukana. They help bring attention to things and show passion.

The arts are an important part of Māori culture. They are meaningful and fun for people to participate in. They are also fun to watch and look at.

I hope you've enjoyed reading about my culture and that you learned something new. What topics should I focus on next week? Food, language, or legends? Let me know in the comments what you are interested in learning about!

—Kaia

Name: ______________________ Date: ______________

Directions: Read "Kaia's Blog." Then, answer the questions.

1. How are *performing* arts different from *visual* arts?
   - (A) They share a rich culture.
   - (B) They are done on canvases.
   - (C) They include sound and movement.
   - (D) They have stunning designs and patterns.

2. How does the image affect the text?
   - (A) It gives the reader little information.
   - (B) It shows the reader how to make each piece of art.
   - (C) It shows Kaia's enthusiasm for her culture.
   - (D) It shows examples of described patterns.

3. What do you do when you *dive into* something?
   - (A) give it away
   - (B) show it to others
   - (C) start it with enthusiasm
   - (D) believe it is true

4. What is the meaning of *Indigenous*?
   - (A) difficult
   - (B) native to
   - (C) regular
   - (D) similar to

5. What cultural or traditional artwork have you seen or learned about? Describe it.

____
____
____
____
____
____
____
____
____

 © Shell Education

Name: ______________________________ Date: ________________

Directions: Closely read these texts. Then, summarize each of the texts.

Close-Reading Texts

The Māori	Kaia's Blog
The Māori (MAU-ree) are Indigenous (in-DIH-juh-nuhs) people of New Zealand. That means they were the first people to live there. The Māori are Polynesian like the Indigenous peoples of Hawai‘i. Nobody knows when Māori people first came to New Zealand. But it is known how they got there. They came to New Zealand in canoes. They came from other parts of the Pacific. The Māori were very skilled sailors.	One type of performance is the *haka*. The haka is a ceremonial dance performed in a group. It's done this way to signify the unity of the tribe. It also shows strength and pride of the tribe. Another performance is *waitata-a-ringa*. Performers sing while moving their hands quickly when they perform. They do this to represent water, wind, and heat. An important part of kapa haka is the facial expressions made by the performers. These expressions are called *pukana*. They help bring attention to things. They can also be used to show passion.

"The Māori" Summary

____

____

____

____

____

"Kaia's Blog" Summary

____

____

____

____

____

Name: ______________________ Date: ______________

Directions: Closely read these texts. Then, compare the texts. Think about things such as genre, language, structure, and purpose.

Close-Reading Texts

Preparing for the Festival	Auckland, New Zealand
It was an exciting week for Kaia and her family. They were helping volunteer for the annual summer festival at their local community center in Auckland. Kaia's family was Māori, and they often volunteered for this event. It was a weekend filled with special introductions, music, dancing, and feasts. During this time, people in her community met with tourists from around the world, talked about their cultures, and had a good time.	Auckland is the biggest city in New Zealand. Auckland is sometimes called "the city of sails." That is because it is famous for its sailing and yacht races. Auckland is also home to Sky Tower. Sky Tower is the tallest building in the Southern Hemisphere. People can go to the top of Sky Tower and see for miles around. More fun things to do around the city include going on dolphin or whale-watching tours, visiting the zoo, or following the many bike paths. Plus, there are countless stores and restaurants.

Preparing for the Festival **Auckland, New Zealand**

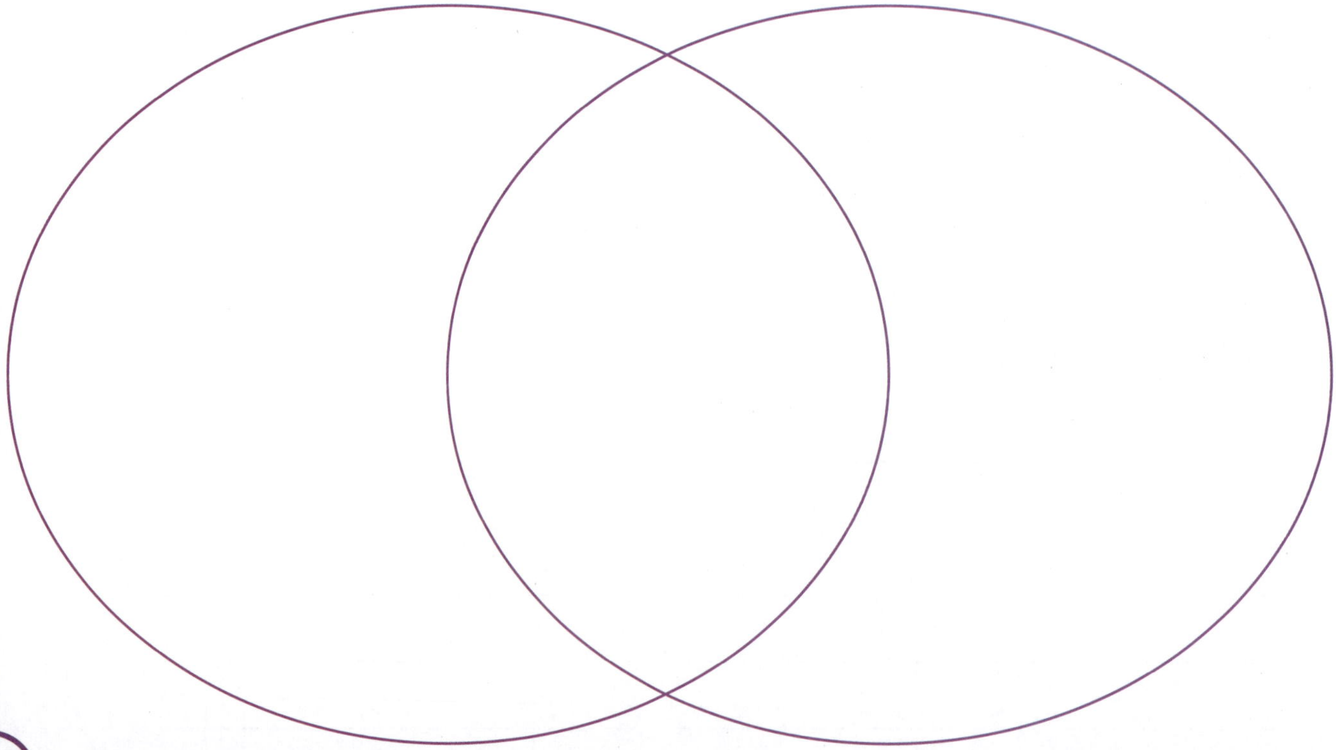

 © Shell Education

Name: ______________________________ Date: ______________

Directions: Reread the texts from this unit. Then, respond to the prompt.

Explain what you find to be the most interesting aspect of the Māori culture. Introduce the topic clearly, state an opinion, and provide logically ordered reasons that are supported by facts and details.

© Shell Education

Name: ______________________ Date: ____________

Directions: Write a blog post about a family or cultural tradition you participate in or know about. Be sure to include illustrations to support your ideas.

11:11 100%

MY BLOG

____

____

____

____

____

____

____

____

____

____

____

____

____

____

____

____

____

____

____

____

© Shell Education

Name: ______________________ Date: ______________

Directions: Read the text, and answer the questions.

As You Read

Underline facts that explain why size does not necessarily factor into winning a Judo match.

Judo: A Martial Art

Judo is one of the many types of martial arts. It is a sport that does not use weapons. Instead, judo uses holds and body movements. In that way, it is a little like karate. Judo was started in 1882 by Dr. Jigoro Kano. He studied martial arts in Japan and developed judo from them. People do not have to be big and strong to learn judo because it is about timing. It is also about movement and skill. Judo experts can win competitions even when their opponents are bigger. They know that timing and skill are more important than size. Anyone can learn judo. There are classes for people of all ages and all ability levels. It is even an Olympic sport.

1. Which reason supports that judo is a little like karate?
   - (A) Judo started in Japan.
   - (B) People cannot take classes to learn judo.
   - (C) Judo uses holds and body movements.
   - (D) Timing is more important than size in judo.

2. Which phrase supports that an *expert* is *someone who is good at doing something*?
   - (A) to be big and strong
   - (B) of all ages and abilities
   - (C) more important than size
   - (D) even when their opponents are bigger

3. Which is the root word in *competitions*?
   - (A) compete
   - (B) competitive
   - (C) competitor
   - (D) petition

4. Which subordinating conjunction explains why anyone can learn judo?
   - (A) even little children
   - (B) instead of weapons
   - (C) because it is about timing
   - (D) even when their opponents are bigger

Name: ______________________________ Date: ________________

Directions: Read the text, and answer the questions.

As You Read

Underline key words related to fencing.

Fencing: An Olympic Sport

Fencing is a sport in which people use a special kind of sword and wear protective clothes. Fencing started in France, so most of the words used in fencing are French. Fencing is an Olympic sport. The object of a fencing match is to touch your opponent with your weapon as many times as possible. Whoever gets the most touches is the winner. There are several fencing moves that fencers have to learn. For example, fencers learn how to try to touch their opponents and how to defend themselves against an opponent's touch. They learn how to move around, both backward and forward. Have you ever seen a movie that had a sword fight? The actors who used the swords probably learned to fence!

1. How is fencing related to sword fighting?
   - (A) Both fencing and sword fighting are Olympic sports.
   - (B) Actors who sword-fight likely learned fencing.
   - (C) Fencing started in France, but sword fighting started in Rome.
   - (D) Fencing takes a lot of practice, but sword fighting can be learned quickly.

2. What do fencers have to learn?
   - (A) how to speak French
   - (B) how to wear special clothing
   - (C) how to get to matches
   - (D) how to touch their opponent

3. Which example of figurative language may be used to describe fencing?
   - (A) to be "on the fence" as to when to attack
   - (B) to "go out on a limb" when joining a fencing match
   - (C) to "be on cloud nine" when winning a fencing match
   - (D) to look to "the other side of the fence" for a better fencing sword

4. What is the best meaning of the word *object* in the text?
   - (A) a thing
   - (B) the focus
   - (C) the goal
   - (D) to protest

 © Shell Education

Name: ______________________________ Date: ______________

Directions: Read the text, and answer the questions.

As You Read

Place a star beside information that explains how to row.

Rowing: A Team Sport

If you like to be out on the water, you might enjoy the sport of rowing. Rowing is popular wherever there are large bodies of water, such as lakes, rivers and oceans. It is one of the oldest Olympic sports. In rowing, teams of people race one another in special boats. To move their boats, rowers sit facing backward on special seats in their boat. They use paddles called *oars* that are designed for rowing and are attached to the boat. Rowers have to have a lot of strength and work together as a team to pull their oars. Each person on the team has to row in the right direction at exactly the right time. Otherwise, the boat will not move forward smoothly. Rowing can be good exercise for people because it makes arm and back muscles strong. Rowing also helps people strengthen their leg muscles. Rowing can be a fun and fast workout!

1. Where is rowing done?
   - (A) on a field
   - (B) in a gymnasium
   - (C) in a stadium
   - (D) on waterways

2. What special paddles do rowers use?
   - (A) boats
   - (B) seats
   - (C) oars
   - (D) rows

3. Why do rowers have to work together as a team? ______________________________

____

____

4. Compare rowing to another water sport. ______________________________

____

____

____

Name: ______________________ Date: ______________

As You Read

Circle time-order words that indicate a sequence of events.

The Summer Olympic Games

Every four years, a special sporting event occurs in the world. Athletes from all over the world gather together. They compete against each other in their sports and try to win medals. This special event is the Summer Olympic Games. It is also called the *Olympiad*. Many sports are a part of the Olympics. Athletes row, fence, and ride horses. They swim, run, and play soccer. Judo and boxing are also part of the Summer Olympics. So are baseball and gymnastics. The Olympics have a long history and have been held in many places.

The Olympics were created long ago. Nearly 3,000 years ago in Ancient Greece, people got together every four years. They raced and boxed. They competed to see who could throw a spear the farthest. They competed in other events, too. But after many years, the Greeks stopped having the games. For a long time, there were no games.

In 1896, the modern Olympics began. The first modern Olympic Games were held in Athens. Athens is the capital of Greece. Since 1900, the games have been held every four years. The one exception is 2020 due to the COVID-19 pandemic. And the games have only been cancelled three times: in 1916, 1940, and 1944. In those years, the games could not be held because of World War I and World War II.

Many locations around the world have hosted the Olympics. Each year, the games are held in a different city. Cities that want to host the Olympics have to apply to host the games. They apply to a special group of people. This group is the International Olympic Committee. The group decides which city will get the games. Some of the cities include Paris, Los Angeles, Rome, and Rio de Janeiro. Most recently, the Olympics were held in Tokyo.

People around the world look forward to the Summer Olympics. Wherever they are held, millions of people watch them!

© Shell Education

Name: ______________________ Date: ______________

Directions: Read "The Summer Olympic Games." Then, answer the questions.

1. Which event happens first?
   - (A) The Olympic Games are held.
   - (B) Cities apply to the International Olympic Committee.
   - (C) Cities decide that they want to host the Olympic Games.
   - (D) The committee decides where the Olympic Games will be.

2. What is true of modern-day Olympics?
   - (A) The Games are held every six years.
   - (B) The Games are always held in Greece.
   - (C) The Games are held all over the world.
   - (D) The Games do not include games from the first Olympics.

3. How is this text different from the text in first three days of this week?
   - (A) This text compares different Olympic Games.
   - (B) This text gives opinions about the Olympic Games.
   - (C) This text explains how athletes prepare for the Games.
   - (D) This text lists many Olympic Games instead of just one.

4. Why were the first modern Olympic Games most likely held in Athens?
   - (A) The first Olympics were held by the Greeks.
   - (B) Athens offered more site-seeing options for visitors.
   - (C) People can easily travel to Athens compared to other cities.
   - (D) Athens had more space to hold several competitions at one time.

5. List events related to the Ol ympics in chronological order.

Event 1	The first Olympics were held in Greece nearly 3,000 years ago.
Event 2	
Event 3	
Event 4	

Name: ______________________ Date: ______________

Directions: Reread "The Summer Olympic Games." Then, respond to the prompt.

Write a story as if you were a spectator at either the ancient or modern Olympics. Develop your story with descriptive details and a clear sequence of events.

© Shell Education

Name: ______________________ Date: ______________

Directions: Read the text, and answer the questions.

As You Read

Place a plus sign (+) beside positive ideas related to the pool.
Place a minus sign (–) beside negative ideas related to the pool.

Saturday Swimming

Sammy and her family went to the community pool every Saturday during the summer. It was something she looked forward to all week. She loved being outside and talking to her friends. But most importantly, she loved being in the water. She enjoyed any activity that took place in water. Whether it was floating, racing her friends, or jumping into the deep end, she always had a good time. She loved how refreshing the water felt and how it made her feel weightless. To her, being in the water was the most peaceful place.

Sammy only had one gripe with swimming, and it was that she never felt like she was great at it. She knew how to keep herself afloat, and she could kind of do a sidestroke, but that was about it. Plus, she never won any of the races against her friends, and she always felt that her form was awkward.

1. Why is the setting important to the story?
   - (A) The pool is open all year long.
   - (B) Saturday is the only day the pool is open.
   - (C) The pool is the only place Sammy is happy.
   - (D) The pool is a place to get fresh air while swimming.

2. What is a synonym for *gripe*?
   - (A) complaint
   - (B) fear
   - (C) image
   - (D) spectacle

3. What disappoints Sammy?
   - (A) She cannot swim in the rain.
   - (B) She is not a strong swimmer.
   - (C) Her friends don't want to race her.
   - (D) Her muscles cramp when she swims too hard.

4. What is a good metaphor for Sammy?
   - (A) Sammy is a fish.
   - (B) Sammy is a pool.
   - (C) Sammy is a snail.
   - (D) Sammy is a waterfall.

Name: ______________________ Date: ____________

Directions: Read the text, and answer the questions.

As You Read

Circle words that show how the characters are feeling.

Sunday Swim Class

Sammy's family decided to skip the pool one Saturday, and they went on Sunday instead. When they arrived, they found some chairs and put down their towels. Sammy was about to head into the water when she realized that the shallow section of the pool was closed off to the public.

"Hey Mom, what do you think they're doing?" Sammy asked.

"Oh, I think it's for a class that teaches people how to properly swim," her mom said. "It looks like they are practicing specific strokes."

Sammy gasped in excitement. "I definitely want to do that!" she exclaimed.

"Alright, we can get some details and ask about signing up," her mom said.

Sammy was already imagining herself as an amazing swimmer, winning races left and right. Before they left the pool that day, Sammy was signed up for next Sunday's class.

1. How is the setting of this story different from "Saturday Swimming"?
   - (A) On Sunday, the pool is closed to guests.
   - (B) On Sunday, the pool is open fewer hours.
   - (C) On Sunday, the pool has more lifeguards.
   - (D) On Sunday, the pool offers swimming classes.

2. What is a synonym for *intrigued*?
   - (A) baffled
   - (B) interested
   - (C) open
   - (D) snug

3. What does Sammy look forward to next weekend?
   - (A) diving
   - (B) swim classes
   - (C) picnicking at the pool
   - (D) swimming with friends

4. What is Sammy's main goal?
   - (A) to learn to dive
   - (B) to swim with her friends
   - (C) to win swimming races
   - (D) to swim longer at the pool

 © Shell Education

Name: ______________________ Date: ______________

Directions: Read the text, and answer the questions.

As You Read

Write a ∞ wherever you make connections to the text.

Sammy's First Swim Class

Sammy was feeling nervous about her first swimming class. She felt excited, too, but she was worried about being the only mediocre swimmer there.

"No one is going to be that great at first," her father reassured her. "The lessons are supposed to make you better. And we will be there cheering you on from the sidelines. It will be like any other day at the pool!" This was enough to calm some of Sammy's anxiety. Plus, her excitement had kicked in at this point.

At the pool, Sammy walked over toward the instructor. She almost asked her parents to come with her but decided against it at the last minute.

"Hello everyone!" the instructor greeted everyone. "We still have about five minutes until class starts, but I'll be right here if you have any questions."

Sammy smiled at the instructor and walked to the shallow end of the pool, preparing for the lesson.

1. Why doesn't Sammy ask her parents to come with her?
   - (A) She wants to be brave.
   - (B) She doesn't like her parents.
   - (C) Her parents would yell at her.
   - (D) Her parents embarrass her.

2. What does *mediocre* mean?
   - (A) friendly
   - (B) just okay
   - (C) marvelous
   - (D) terrible

3. Why is Sammy both nervous and excited? ______________________

____

____

4. What is something you wish you were better at? Why? ______________

____

____

Name: ______________________________ Date: ____________________

As You Read

Number the steps to performing a side stroke in swimming.

Great Form!

"Alright swimmers, let's get started," the instructor said. "For our first exercise, let's have everyone exit the pool!"

Sammy glanced at the other kids, who looked just as confused as she was.

Once everyone was poolside, she continued, "Today's focus is the side stroke. We'll start with the leg movements. Everyone lie down on your left side."

Sammy was feeling unsure of herself, but she followed directions.

"Now, extend your left arm above your head, and rest your head on the upper part of your arm. And face your palm down on the ground."

"Perfect!" the instructor said. "Now, place your right hand across your chest and onto the floor in front of you for balance."

"Okay, now bend your knees to a 90-degree angle," she said. "Then, pull your knees toward your chest, and kick your legs in the opposite direction. Your top leg should kick out to the front as your bottom leg kicks back. As you straighten both legs, bring them back together to the starting position."

Sammy held her breath and tried really hard to follow the instructions.

Sammy heard the instructor yell, "Great form, Sammy!"

Sammy felt proud of herself as the class continued to practice the leg movements on both sides. Then, they practiced the corresponding arm movements. Finally, they practiced working their arms and legs simultaneously.

"Nice work, everybody," the instructor said. "Now, let's add some water."

The class attempted the same techniques in the pool. Eventually, they even held some races. Sammy surprised herself by coming in first during one of the races.

"Your daughter is a natural," the instructor said to Sammy's parents. "She's like a fish!"

"That's incredible!" Sammy's mom cheered.

Later that night, the family discussed Sammy's new passion over dinner.

"So, Sammy, do you want to continue swim lessons? You could also compete in official swim meets," her mom said.

"Yes, that sounds amazing!" Sammy said. "Olympics, here I come!"

"Go for the gold!" her mom and dad yelled.

 © Shell Education

Name: ______________________________ Date: ______________

Directions: Read "Great Form!" Then, answer the questions.

1. How do Sammy's parents react to the idea of the Olympics?

- (A) They both think it's not a good idea.
- (B) Her mom is excited, but her dad is doubtful.
- (C) They both encourage Sammy to have that dream.
- (D) Her mom is cautious, but her dad is enthusiastic.

2. How does Sammy's mood change?

- (A) At first she is afraid, then she becomes terrified.
- (B) At first she is nervous, then she becomes uncertain.
- (C) At first she is unsure, then she becomes confident.
- (D) At first she is excited, then she becomes less confident.

3. What is another word for *corresponding*?

- (A) communicating
- (B) matching
- (C) personalizing
- (D) rationalizing

4. Who must perform movements *simultaneously*?

- (A) dancers
- (B) painters
- (C) sculptors
- (D) writers

5. Summarize the steps to perform the side stroke.

1.	
2.	
3.	
4.	
5.	
6.	

© Shell Education

Name: ______________________ Date: ______________

Directions: Reread "Great Form!" Then, respond to the prompt.

Think about something you can teach someone else to do. Write clear steps for another person to follow to successfully do this thing. Link ideas using words, phrases, and clauses.

© Shell Education

Name: ________________________________ Date: ______________

An Interview with Sammy

Interviewer: How old were you when you first started swimming?

Sammy: I first started to take it seriously as a sport when I was around 11 years old. That's when I joined the local swim team. That same year, I went to my first swim meet. I placed second in my main event and third in my second event. My main event is the 100-meter freestyle and my second event is the 100-meter backstroke.

Interviewer: Did you always have the Olympics in mind as your goal?

Sammy: Not always. My parents really emphasized that I do swimming for fun. My first swim instructor said I should consider it in the future. I tried to follow the idea of taking everything one step at a time. I realized that competing was good motivation to practice and get better. Then, I started winning first place more in high school. That's when the idea of going to the Olympics seemed more achievable.

Interviewer: Who helped you achieve this goal? Did you have any family members or friends who supported or encouraged you?

Sammy: Definitely! My parents were always so supportive. They would wake up early to bring me to my practices and meets, and they made sure that I had a healthy breakfast and was ready to take on the day. My siblings and friends were also very supportive. They often came to watch me compete. I'm incredibly grateful for their support over the years.

Interviewer: Tell me about the first time you qualified for the Olympics. How did it feel?

Sammy: I was ecstatic, of course! It didn't feel real until a day or two later. That's when it sunk in that my years of hard work had paid off. Even now, after attending three different Olympics, I still get overjoyed when I find out I've qualified again. It's really one of the best feelings I've ever experienced.

Interviewer: What is one piece of advice you'd like to give young athletes who are dreaming of one day going to the Olympics themselves?

Sammy: It takes determination. Sometimes, it seems like all you're doing is practicing. But the opportunity of competing in the Olympics makes it worth it. If it's something you love to do, then you should go for it!

Interviewer: Thank you for taking the time for this interview, Sammy. I really appreciate it and I know your fans will love to read your responses!

Name: ______________________ Date: ______________

Directions: Read "An Interview with Sammy." Then, answer the questions.

1. How is the language Sammy uses in the interview different to that in the story, "Great Form!"?
   - (A) She speaks more formally during the interview.
   - (B) She speaks more informally during the interview.
   - (C) She speaks more cautiously during the interview.
   - (D) She speaks more solemnly during the interview.

2. To whom does Sammy give credit for her support?
   - (A) her teachers
   - (B) her swim coach
   - (C) friends and family
   - (D) her Olympics coach

3. Which of the following has the closest meaning to *ecstatic*?
   - (A) happy
   - (B) pleased
   - (C) satisfied
   - (D) thrilled

4. What is a lesson from the interview?
   - (A) Listen to others when setting goals.
   - (B) Setting unrealistic goals will motivate you to work harder.
   - (C) With hard work and determination, you can achieve anything.
   - (D) Rely on family and friends to get you through the tough times.

5. Describe a goal you have and how you might achieve it.

____

____

____

____

____

____

____

____

 © Shell Education

Name: ______________________________ Date: ______________

Directions: Closely read these texts. Complete the graphic organizer.

Close-Reading Texts

Great Form!	An Interview with Sammy
"Your daughter is a natural," the instructor said to Sammy's parents after class. She's like a fish!" "That's incredible!" Sammy's mom cheered. Later that night, the family discussed Sammy's new passion over dinner. "So, Sammy, do you want to continue swim lessons? You could also compete in official swim meets," her mom said. "Yes, that sounds amazing!" Sammy said. "Olympics, here I come!"	**Interviewer:** Did you always have the Olympics in mind as your goal? **Sammy:** Not always. My parents really emphasized that I do swimming for fun. My first swim instructor said I should consider it in the future. I tried to follow the idea of taking everything one step at a time. I realized that competing was good motivation to practice and get better. Then, I started winning first place more in high school. That's when the idea of going to the Olympics seemed more achievable.

	Great Form!	An Interview with Sammy
Point of View	*(circle one)* first person second person third person	*(circle one)* first person second person third person
	I know this because	I know this because
Description of Events		

Name: ______________________________ Date: ______________

Directions: Closely read these texts. Compare fencing and rowing.

Close-Reading Texts

Fencing: An Olympic Sport	Rowing: A Team Sport
The object of a fencing match is to touch your opponent with your weapon as many times as possible. Whoever gets the most touches is the winner. There are several fencing moves that fencers have to learn. For example, fencers learn how to try to touch their opponents and how to defend themselves against an opponent's touch. They learn how to move around, both backward and forward.	To move their boats, rowers sit facing backward on special seats in their boats. They use paddles called oars that are designed for rowing and are attached to the boat. The oars push the boat through the water. Rowers have to work together as a team. Each person on the team has to row in the right direction at exactly the right time. Otherwise, the boat will not move forward.

Fencing	Rowing
Both	

© Shell Education

Name: ______________________________ Date: ______________

Directions: Think about the texts from this unit. Then, respond to the prompt.

Imagine that you are Sammy from the story. You just went to your first swimming lesson. Write a diary entry about your experience. Use descriptive words and phrases and sensory details to tell about your experience. Draw a picture.

Name: ______________________________ Date: ______________

Directions: What would you ask a famous athlete? Write an interview between the two of you. As the interviewer, you ask the questions. The person you interview will answer them. Write your interview as a script, similar to the interview on page 149.

 © Shell Education

Name: ______________________________ Date: ______________

Directions: Read the text, and answer the questions.

As You Read

Circle one main idea of the text. Underline the details that support this main idea.

The Importance of Nurses

Nurses are very important healthcare professionals. Nurses have a variety of tasks to perform at their jobs. They treat patients, teach people how to stay healthy, and create plans for patient care. Many nurses go to college or specialized schools to learn nursing. Then, they choose what kind of nursing they want to do. Today, they have many choices. Some places they work include hospitals, doctors' offices, clinics, and schools. Other nurses are considered to be visiting nurses. This means they go to the homes of people who cannot get to a doctor's office. Nursing is a career that takes a lot of skill, practice, and specialized learning, but it is also very rewarding.

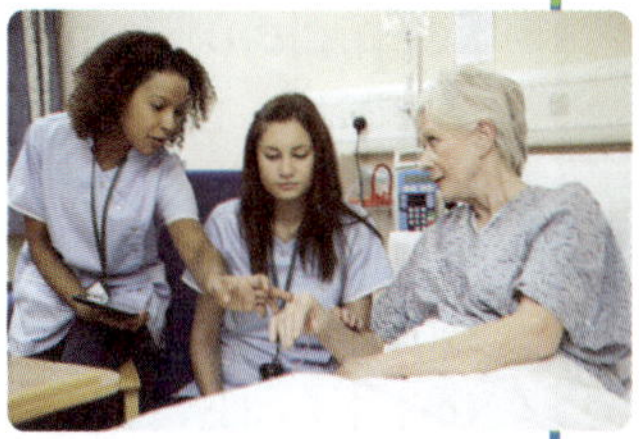

1. Which of the following is **not** listed as a reason why nurses need to know many things?
   - (A) They treat patients.
   - (B) They build hospitals.
   - (C) They create plans for patient care.
   - (D) They teach people how to stay healthy.

2. What does the author mean by nursing "is also very rewarding?"
   - (A) Nursing is challenging.
   - (B) Nurses feel pleased about their jobs.
   - (C) Nurses get rewards.
   - (D) Nurses can be reimbursed for the cost of college.

3. What is another word for *choices*?
   - (A) options
   - (B) rules
   - (C) tasks
   - (D) thoughts

4. What does the conjunction *but* in the last sentence tell you?
   - (A) Doctors rely on the nurses they work with.
   - (B) Some types of nursing are more satisfying than others.
   - (C) Some people may not find nursing rewarding.
   - (D) Nursing is worth the time needed to learn it.

Name: ______________________________ Date: ______________

Directions: Read the text, and answer the questions.

As You Read

Place a star beside facts that describe nursing long ago. Place an exclamation point beside facts that describe nursing today.

The History of Nursing

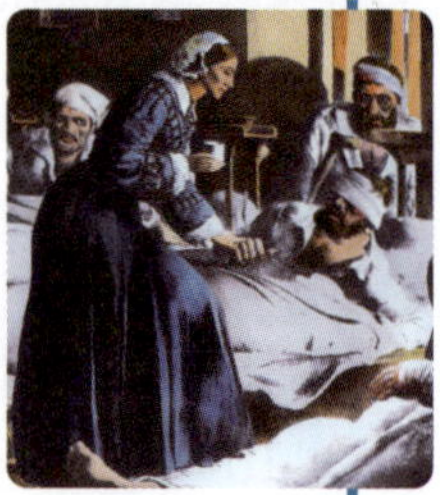

The role of nurses has changed over time. Modern-day nurses are well-educated professionals who have many skills. They can be women or men. But things were not always this way. Many years ago, nurses were not skilled. They simply fed patients, helped them keep clean, and kept them warm. Nurses sometimes helped doctors, but they were not treated with respect. And only women could be nurses.

Florence Nightingale helped change nursing forever. Nightingale was an English nurse. She lived during the 1800s. In 1853, the Crimean War began. During this war, England went to war with Turkey. Nightingale took a team of nurses to Turkey. She and her team helped the British soldiers. She insisted that nurses should be respected. She wanted nurses to get an education. After the war, she set up a school just for nurses. She made an important impact on the career of nursing.

1. What is the main difference between nursing long ago and nursing today?
   - Ⓐ Nurses are respected.
   - Ⓑ Nurses are not educated.
   - Ⓒ Nurses work with doctors.
   - Ⓓ Only women can be nurses.

2. What is the meaning of the word *skilled*?
   - Ⓐ *helpful* and *caring*
   - Ⓑ *smart* and *carefree*
   - Ⓒ *trained* and *practiced*
   - Ⓓ *important* and *reliable*

3. Which prepositional phrase describes when Florence Nightingale lived?
   - Ⓐ to Turkey
   - Ⓑ with respect
   - Ⓒ after the war
   - Ⓓ during the 1800's

4. What does the word *insisted* tell you about Florence Nightingale?
   - Ⓐ She was afraid.
   - Ⓑ She was caring.
   - Ⓒ She was helpful.
   - Ⓓ She was determined.

© Shell Education

Name: ______________________ Date: ____________

Directions: Read the text, and answer the questions.

As You Read

Underline information that is new to you. Put a star beside information you already knew.

The Red Cross

Sometimes, large storms or earthquakes strike. Volcanoes might erupt. Or there might be floods or other natural disasters. When those things happen, many people get hurt or need help. Who helps in times of danger and disaster?

The Red Cross is an organization that exists to help people when disaster strikes. The Red Cross is a volunteer group that sends people into an area to help. Those volunteers treat people who need healthcare. Volunteers also provide food, clothes, water, and shelter. Sometimes, rescue dogs join the Red Cross volunteers.

Many countries around the world have Red Cross groups. When there is a disaster in another country, Red Cross groups can work with each other. They can send volunteers and other types of aid, such as food and water.

1. What is true about the Red Cross?
   - (A) It is only in the United States.
   - (B) There are many Red Cross groups around the world.
   - (C) People who work for the Red Cross must work alone.
   - (D) People who work for the Red Cross must rescue people.

2. The Red Cross is a *volunteer group*. What does this mean?
   - (A) People hope disasters will strike.
   - (B) People travel the world to help others.
   - (C) People give their time without pay.
   - (D) People work together to get the job done.

3. When are times the Red Cross may be called upon to help? ____________________

____

4. How might the Red Cross help you at some point? ____________________

____

Name: ______________________________ Date: ______________

As You Read

Identify at least one cause-and-effect relationship. Circle the cause. Underline the effect.

Clara Barton

Whenever there is a disaster, there are people who may need help. The Red Cross is there to help them. The Red Cross is a group of volunteers who go to places where disasters have occurred. The group provides food, water, shelter, and medicine. The Red Cross has been responsible for saving many people's lives.

The American Red Cross was started in 1881 by Clara Barton. Barton was born on December 25, 1821. She knew she was good at being a nurse and helping people from the time she was a child. When she was 11 years old, her brother David became very ill, and Barton nursed him back to health. Later, she became a teacher and started her own school. But then the Civil War came, and everything changed for Barton. She saw that the soldiers needed blankets, clothes, food, and other supplies. So she and some other people gave them what they needed. Then, she led a team of nurses who helped the soldiers. Barton worked very hard and became very famous for everything that she did to help the soldiers.

Barton worked so hard that she became ill. Her doctors advised her to take a long trip and rest. So, Barton went to Europe. But she did not rest. Instead, she learned about the Red Cross. Some countries had groups of volunteers that assisted people who needed help. Barton wanted to have the same kind of organization in the United States. So, when she came back to America, she worked with other people and created the American Red Cross. For 23 years, she was its president.

Barton did many other things in her life, too. For example, she worked very hard to give women the right to vote. She also worked hard to create a system to find missing people. Clara Barton died in 1912, but the work she did changed the United States and has saved millions of lives.

© Shell Education

Name: ______________________ Date: ____________

Directions: Read "Clara Barton." Then, answer the questions.

1. What is true about the American Red Cross?

- (A) It was started in 1821.
- (B) It was founded by Clara Barton.
- (C) It was around during the American Civil War.
- (D) It was the first Red Cross organization in the world.

2. Which detail supports the idea that Barton was good at nursing?

- (A) She started her own school.
- (B) She fought in the American Civil War.
- (C) She helped her brother survive a terrible illness.
- (D) She worked with people in Europe to learn about the Red Cross.

3. What happened as a result of Barton's trip to Europe?

- (A) She learned how to be a nurse.
- (B) She won an award for her bravery.
- (C) She helped soldiers in battles there.
- (D) She started the American Red Cross.

4. Which of the following is an example of a shelter?

- (A) a pizza
- (B) a rainstorm
- (C) a sweater
- (D) a tent

5. Write an effect for each cause from the text.

Cause	Effect
Barton saw that soldiers needed blankets, clothes, food, and more.	
Barton worked hard to help Civil War soldiers.	
Barton's doctors advised she take a trip when she fell ill.	

Name: ______________________ Date: ______________

Directions: Reread "The History of Nursing" and "Clara Barton." Then, respond to the prompt.

Explain how nursing has changed over the years. Use information and examples from both texts to support your ideas.

© Shell Education

Name: ______________________________ Date: ______________

Directions: Read the text, and answer the questions.

As You Read

Circle the problem in the story. Underline the solution.

Emily and the Earthquake

Emily and her dad were inside their house when an earthquake began. They dropped to the floor, darted under the kitchen table, and held on until it was over.

Finally, the shaking stopped. When Emily looked around, she noticed they were surrounded by concrete and wood pieces from their collapsed house. Luckily, the table had been sturdy enough to protect them both.

"Is anyone in there?" a person's voice bellowed.

"Yes!" Emily's dad yelled. "There are two of us and we're under a table."

"Are you hurt?" the person asked.

"We're fine, we just can't seem to find a way out," Emily's dad said. The person told them to hold on for a few moments. She could hear the people above starting to use some tools and move things around. When the rescuers pulled her and her dad out of the remnants of the house, Emily thanked them. She was so grateful for the paramedics and other volunteers in her community.

1. Why does Emily duck under a table?
   - (A) to tidy up
   - (B) for protection
   - (C) to hide from her sister
   - (D) to pretend to be in a fort

2. What is the result of the earthquake?
   - (A) The house mostly collapses.
   - (B) Some neighbors left in a hurry.
   - (C) Emily's pet runs away.
   - (D) The neighborhood is destroyed.

3. Which word is closest in meaning to *bellow*?
   - (A) announce
   - (B) say
   - (C) shout
   - (D) utter

4. Which word uses the Greek root *para-* similar to the word *paramedic*?
   - (A) parallel
   - (B) paralegal
   - (C) paranoid
   - (D) parant

Name: ______________________________ Date: ________________

Directions: Read the text, and answer the questions.

As You Read

Circle ways the Red Cross provided assistance.

Zaharah and the Tornado

Zaharah's family had hunkered down in their basement after hearing a tornado warning. The concrete walls of the basement kept them safe during the emergency. Once the wind had been quiet for more than 10 minutes, her parents went upstairs to check whether it was safe to come out. Her parents came back down to give the all clear. Everyone went outside to see what had happened. They were in shock as they looked at their neighborhood. They saw that house after house had been damaged! Luckily, no one was hurt, but Zaharah thought that the destruction was heartbreaking.

Soon, some cars drove up the street to help. The people inside were from the Red Cross. They brought some food, water, first aid, and other supplies with them. They provided a shelter location to everyone who needed it. Over the next few months, they even helped fix and rebuild the homes.

Zaharah's family and her neighborhood had been through a terrible ordeal, but they would be okay.

1. What is the result of the tornado?
   - (A) Trees are overturned.
   - (B) Many people are injured.
   - (C) Cars are tossed about.
   - (D) Homes are damaged.

2. How does the Red Cross assist?
   - (A) They round up lost pets.
   - (B) They help clean up debris.
   - (C) They give supplies and support to families in need.
   - (D) They call family and friends of those in need.

3. What is an antonym for *ordeal*?
   - (A) celebration
   - (B) enthusiasm
   - (C) instruction
   - (D) suffering

4. When is a time you might *hunker down*?
   - (A) during a blizzard
   - (B) during a sporting event
   - (C) during a hospital stay
   - (D) during a family get-together

 © Shell Education

Name: ______________________ Date: ______________

Directions: Read the text, and answer the questions.

As You Read

Underline problems that made an impact on Kenyon's family.

Kenyon and the Fire

One night, Kenyon awoke to the smell of smoke and his eyes burning. *Fire,* he realized, *another wildfire this summer!* In a flash, he jumped out of bed and found his parents. They had their essentials already packed in a duffel bag. They rushed out of the house and drove away in their car as fast as they could safely go.

Kenyon and his parents weren't sure where to go at first. The fire seemed like it had spread so quickly that an evacuation center hadn't been set up yet.

"Let's just keep heading out of the mountains," Kenyon's father said.

They were starting to run low on gas, and firetrucks whizzed by them on the road. As they drove past an intersection, they noticed a sign in the ground. It had a Red Cross symbol with the words *EMERGENCY SHELTER.* They followed the sign to the shelter, which was set up in an elementary school gym. They were greeted, given food, water, information about the fire, and cots to rest on.

Kenyon and his family were relieved. They were grateful to have somewhere safe they could rest, eat, and figure out what to do next.

1. How does the Red Cross help Kenyon's family?
   - (A) They take them to safety.
   - (B) They provide medical care.
   - (C) They provide shelter.
   - (D) They give them fire-proof blankets.

2. What is the meaning of *in a flash*?
   - (A) brightly
   - (B) hurriedly
   - (C) slowly
   - (D) thoughtfully

3. Besides the fire, what problem does Kenyon's family face? ______________________

____

4. Why is having an evacuation plan important? ______________________

____

Name: ______________________________ Date: ______________

As You Read

Circle activities the campers will participate in.

Survival Training and Leadership Camp

"Alright, everyone, get in a single file line please," said a camp instructor.

Emily was toward the back of the line. She heard someone say to her, "Hi! I'm Zaharah, what's your name?"

Emily turned around, smiled at her, and replied, "Hi, my name is Emily."

Zaharah continued speaking. "So, what are you most excited for at camp?"

Emily thought for a moment and then replied, "I'm excited to build a first-aid kit and try the blindfolded line activity. It's this exercise where everyone gets in a line, is blindfolded, and follows whoever is in front of them."

A boy nearby appeared to have heard Emily's response.

"Oh, that sounds like interesting team building!" he said. "I just thought we were learning survival skills."

"I think we're doing a mix of activities," Emily said. "What's your name?"

"I'm Kenyon," he said. "So, what made you guys want to come to camp?"

Each of them shared their experience in an emergency. Together, they had experienced an earthquake, a tornado, and a wildfire.

The three campers handed their papers to the leader and grabbed their identification badges. They promised to meet up the next day.

The next day, all the campers met in the grass outside the cabins. Kenyon, Emily, and Zaharah found themselves lined up next to one another, and they waved. A camp leader with a megaphone walked in front of the lines of children.

"Good morning, young campers! My name is Andy! Are we ready to have fun?"

"Yes!" one camper said from the back of the line.

Andy squinted his eyes and put his hand up to his ear as if he couldn't hear.

"I know it's early, but let's try that again," he said. "Are we ready to have fun?!"

"Yes!" the campers yelled ecstatically and in unison.

"That's great!" He paused and looked around until he had everyone's attention. "The next activity is eating breakfast, which you'll surely do well at, too! Then, we will make first aid kits, play a survival game, and then it's team building time!"

Kenyon, Emily, and Zaharah shared looks of anticipation of the week ahead.

© Shell Education

Name: ______________________________ Date: ______________

Directions: Read "Survival Training and Leadership Camp." Then, answer the questions.

1. What is different about the blindfold activity?
   - (A) It requires special equipment.
   - (B) It does not teach survival skills.
   - (C) It will take place in the afternoon.
   - (D) It is meant to make campers uncomfortable.

2. What causes the three campers to bond?
   - (A) They all come from the same town.
   - (B) They all enjoy challenging situations.
   - (C) They all have the same number of siblings.
   - (D) They all experience different but terrifying natural disasters.

3. Why does the author end the instructor's statements with exclamation points?
   - (A) to wake up the campers
   - (B) so everyone can hear them
   - (C) because they are excited about camp
   - (D) to show the campers they mean business

4. Which word uses the prefix mega- in a similar manner as *megaphone*?
   - (A) Megan
   - (B) megastar
   - (C) omega
   - (D) trimegal

5. Compare the characters from the texts this week.

	Disaster Experience	**Response to Camp**
Emily		
Zaharah		
Kenyon		

Name: ______________________________ Date: ______________

Directions: Reread "Survival Training and Leadership Camp." Then, respond to the prompt.

Write a story about a camp you attend where you meet new people. Use dialogue, description, and pacing to tell about the experience.

 © Shell Education

Be Prepared for a Disaster

Emergency Kit Supplies

Disasters can strike at any time. Research disasters that are common or possible in your area. To be prepared, create an emergency kit. Suggested items include but are not limited to:

- battery-powered radio and flashlight
- extra batteries
- first-aid kit
- food and water for at least three days
- hand sanitizer
- toilet paper and paper towels
- change of clothes
- necessary medications
- important documents
- pet supplies

Evacuation Plan

- In an emergency, timing is important. So, practice how long it takes you to gather your emergency supplies and leave your home.
- Designate a place for your family members to meet at you get separated.
- Have an out-of-state family member or friend as a contact to check in with.

Tips for When You Are Staying Home

- Tell someone that you are staying home.
- Use a battery-operated radio to listen for news and updates.
- Stay away from windows, glass doors, and large furniture that is not bolted in place.
- Be prepared for unexpected changes and last-minute evacuation orders.

Remember: Emergencies can be scary, but being prepared and staying calm will help you get through them.

Name: ______________________ Date: ____________

Directions: Read "Be Prepared for a Disaster." Then, answer the questions.

1. What does the infographic describe?
   - Ⓐ where to go in case of an emergency
   - Ⓑ how to pack when you need to evacuate
   - Ⓒ how to be prepared in case of a natural disaster
   - Ⓓ why to trust officials when they tell you to evacuate

2. Why should you alert people if you are staying home?
   - Ⓐ so they can't let others know where you are
   - Ⓑ so they know where to go in case they are evacuated
   - Ⓒ so they know your pets are being taken care of
   - Ⓓ so they can check in with you after the natural disaster

3. What is the meaning of *designate*?
   - Ⓐ assign
   - Ⓑ find
   - Ⓒ replace
   - Ⓓ tell

4. Which idiom means *unexpected*?
   - Ⓐ a fish out of water
   - Ⓑ adding insult to injury
   - Ⓒ out of the blue
   - Ⓓ the last straw

5. What additional items might you pack in your emergency kit?

____

____

____

____

____

____

____

____

____

 © Shell Education

Name: ______________________________ Date: ________________

Directions: Closely read these texts. Then, reread the infographic on page 167. List words that are closely related to natural disasters. Choose two words. Explain to a partner how they relate to natural disasters.

Close-Reading Texts

The Red Cross	Zaharah and the Tornado
Sometimes, large storms or earthquakes strike. Volcanoes might erupt. Or there might be floods or other natural disasters. When those things happen, many people get hurt or need help. Who helps in times of danger and disaster? The Red Cross is an organization that exists to help people when disaster strikes.	Zaharah's family had hunkered down in their basement after hearing a tornado warning. The concrete walls of the basement kept them safe during the emergency. Once the wind had been quiet for more than 10 minutes, her parents went upstairs to check whether it was safe to come out. Her parents came back down to give the all clear. Everyone went outside to see what had happened. They were in shock as they looked at their neighborhood. They saw that house after house had been damaged!

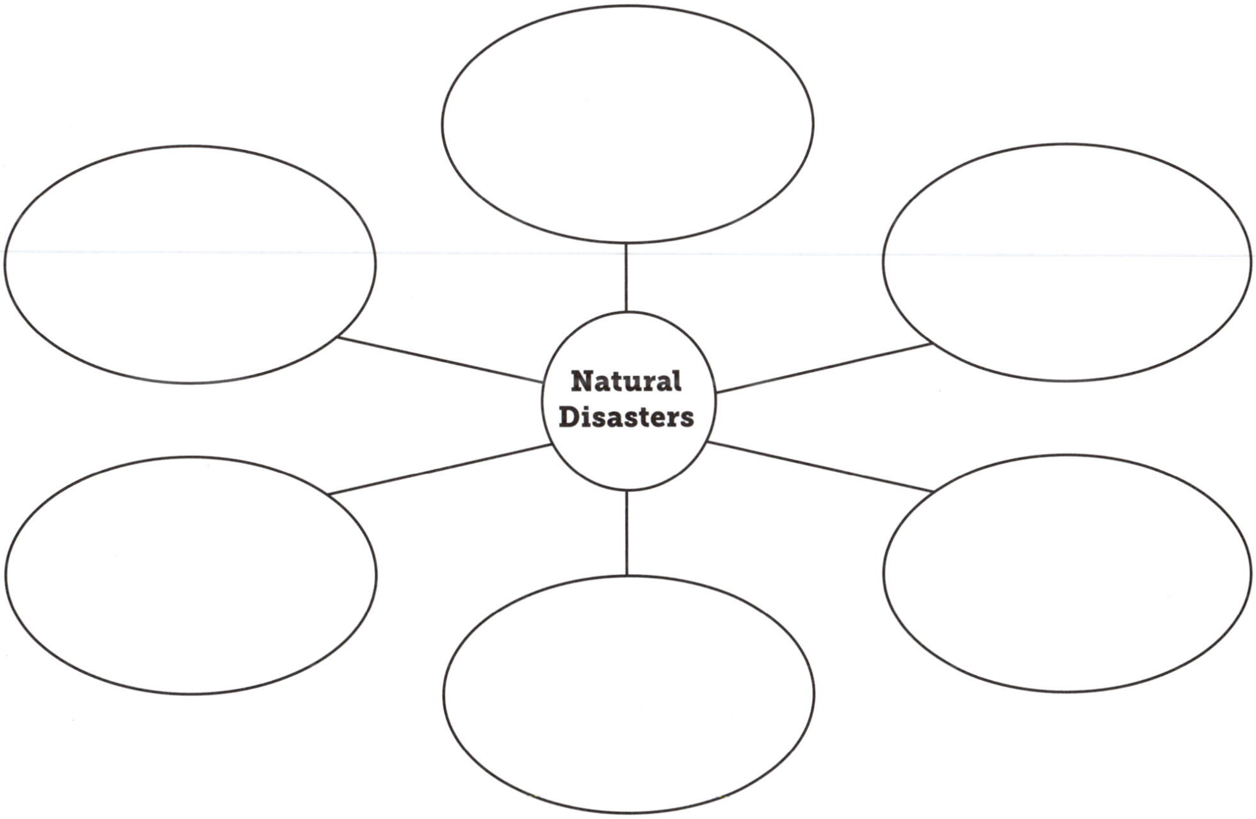

Name: ______________________________ Date: ______________

Directions: Closely read these texts. Then, compare details about how the Red Cross helps those in need.

Close-Reading Texts

The Red Cross	Zaharah and the Tornado
The Red Cross is an organization that exists to help people when disaster strikes. The Red Cross is a volunteer group that sends people into an area to help. Those volunteers treat people who need healthcare. Volunteers also provide food, clothes, water, and shelter. Sometimes, rescue dogs join the Red Cross volunteers.	Soon, some cars drove up the street to help. The people inside were from the Red Cross. They brought some food, water, first aid, and other supplies with them. They provided a shelter location to everyone who needed it. Over the next few months, they even helped fix and rebuild the homes.

The Red Cross	Zaharah and the Tornado

In Both Texts

© Shell Education

Name: ______________________________ Date: ______________

Directions: Reread the texts about nurses, the Red Cross, and natural disasters. Then, respond to the prompt.

Write a thank you letter in which you thank a nurse or Red Cross volunteer for the work they do to help others in natural disasters.

Name: ______________________________ **Date:** ____________________

Directions: Make an infographic about nursing or the Red Cross. Use information from the texts to help you.

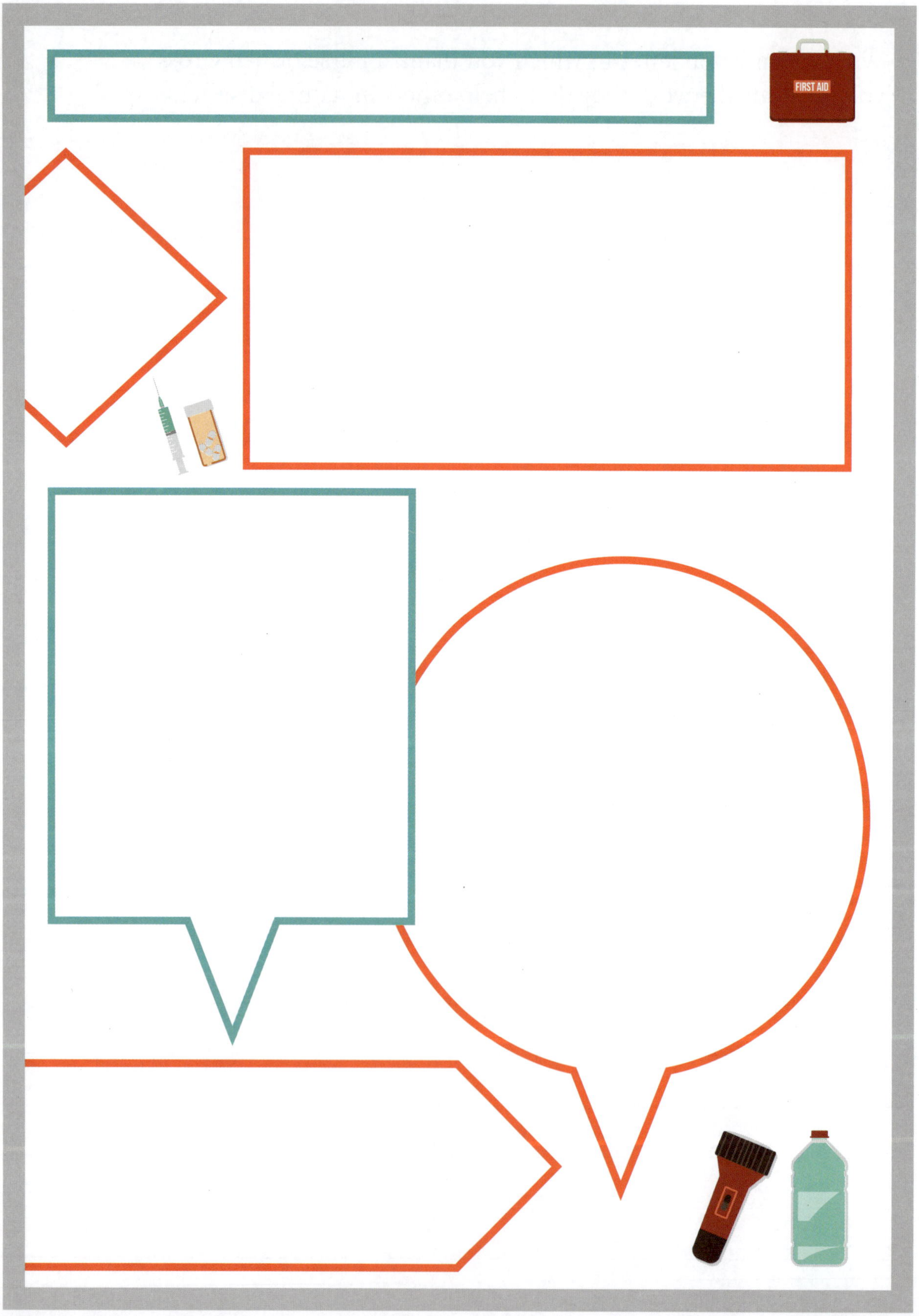

© Shell Education

Name: ______________________________ Date: ______________

Directions: Read the text, and answer the questions.

As You Read

Circle reasons people learn martial arts.

What Are Martial Arts?

Martial arts include many sports and skills that are used for fighting. Many people learn martial arts for self-defense. People also use martial arts for exercise. Doing martial arts is a full body workout. Martial arts can keep your body strong. Some people use meditation while they are doing martial arts. This is because many martial art forms require a person to stay calm while doing movements. They need to keep their attention focused during a fight. Staying focused can make it harder for their opponent to win in a fight or surprise attack. Many forms of martial arts were created in Asia. Some countries where martial arts were created include Japan, China, and Korea.

1. What is one purpose of martial arts?
   - (A) to learn skills to use when fighting
   - (B) to learn to meditate during stressful times
   - (C) to learn movements to help surprise attacks
   - (D) to learn when to predict an enemy will attack

2. Where did many forms of martial arts originate?
   - (A) countries in Africa
   - (B) countries in Asia
   - (C) countries in North America
   - (D) countries in South America

3. How does meditation help a martial artist?
   - (A) They learn to think freely.
   - (B) They learn to stay silent and still.
   - (C) They learn to stay calm and focus.
   - (D) They learn to predict surprise attacks.

4. What is another word for *general*?
   - (A) intense
   - (B) intricate
   - (C) typical
   - (D) unusual

Name: ______________________________ Date: ______________

Directions: Read the text, and answer the questions.

As You Read

Underline details that describe each form of martial arts.

Types of Martial Arts

Some of the most well-known martial arts are karate, kung fu, tae kwon do, and jujitsu. Each of these types are unique in the way they are practiced.

Jujitsu is from Japan, and it is a close combat form of martial art. In close combat, the martial artist may use small weapons. Or, they may use special techniques, such as throws and holds. Throws are movements that get an opponent to the ground. Holds are ways to grab or grip an opponent.

Karate is also a close combat form of martial art. In karate, striking is mostly used. Striking includes punching, kicking, knee strikes, and elbow strikes.

Tae kwon do originated in Korea. It also uses punching and kicking, but tae kwon do focuses on kicking more than karate does.

Kung fu is a general word that refers to Chinese martial arts. There are many types of kung fu, such as Shaolin and tai chi.

1. How do forms of martial arts differ?
   - (A) the way they are taught
   - (B) the way the movements are used
   - (C) where they are practiced
   - (D) the time needed to learn them

2. How are jujitsu and karate alike?
   - (A) They originated in Korea.
   - (B) They are both a close combat sport.
   - (C) They both rely on punching and kicking.
   - (D) They are both general types of martial arts.

3. What is an antonym for *opponent*?
   - (A) ally
   - (B) argument
   - (C) contradiction
   - (D) rival

4. What are the three main movements in martial arts?
   - (A) punching, kicking, and striking
   - (B) gripping, grabbing, and tripping
   - (C) holding, throwing, and striking
   - (D) spinning, throwing, and trapping

© Shell Education

Name: ______________________ Date: ______________

Directions: Read the text, and answer the questions.

As You Read

Circle the names of famous martial artists.
Place a star beside the ones you have heard of.

Famous Martial Artists

Many people practice martial arts, and there are many famous martial artists. Here are just a few of them. One of the most well-known martial artists is Bruce Lee. He is often considered the most influential martial artist of all time. He created his own form of martial arts called *Jeet Kune Do*. Translated, this means "way of the intercepting fist." Bruce Lee was also a famous actor. He showed off his martial arts moves in several famous movies. Another famous martial artist is Jackie Chan. He is also an actor. Like Bruce Lee, he helped make martial arts popular in movies and TV shows. Finally, Chuck Norris is another famous martial artist and actor. He also created his own discipline of martial arts called *Chun Kuk Do*.

1. What do some famous martial artists have in common?
   - (A) They are from Asia.
   - (B) They are also actors.
   - (C) They have their own forms.
   - (D) They have dedicated teachers.

2. What is a *discipline*?
   - (A) design
   - (B) movement
   - (C) specialty
   - (D) weapon

3. What two forms of martial arts are listed in the text? ______________________

____

____

4. Why do you think the famous martial artists you read about also happen to be actors?

____

____

© Shell Education

Name: ______________________ Date: ______________

As You Read

Underline the main idea of each paragraph.
Number details that support each main idea.

A Brief History of Martial Arts

It's difficult to figure out when or how martial arts began. The earliest proof comes from paintings. These paintings come from Ancient Egypt. They show people doing martial arts. The oldest paintings are from 3400 BCE. That's more than 5,000 years ago! The term *martial arts* is often linked to Asia. Proof of ancient martial arts has been found in some Asian countries. This includes China, Japan, and India. But Europe, Africa, and the Middle East also have proof of ancient martial arts.

In China, martial arts have taken many forms over time. Martial arts were first used as a way for people to hunt for food. People also used martial arts to train soldiers. The earliest proof of martial arts in China comes from roughly 500 BCE. Ancient documents described an early form of hand-to-hand combat. They also described techniques for using force. These were labeled as either "soft" or "hard" movements. One of the most popular modern forms of martial arts comes from China. It is a type of kung fu called Shaolin. There is record of the Shaolin form being used in combat around 600 CE. Martial arts have been an important part of Chinese culture throughout time.

Japanese samurai

There are different types of martial arts in Japan. In this country, martial arts started with the samurai. Samurai were important members of the military. They had special privileges and were the only members of society that were allowed to use weapons. Because martial arts started with samurai, early Japanese martial arts focused on using weapons in their practices. Over time, many different styles developed. This includes some styles that don't use weapons. Jujitsu is one of these styles. Today, Japanese martial arts tend to fall into two categories. The first category refers to martial art styles that were created before 1868. These styles are traditional. Their primary use was for war. The second category refers to styles that were created after 1868. These styles are modern. They are often used for self-improvement. Some people may use them for self-defense.

Modern-day martial arts have come a long way from the styles of the past. Next time you practice a move in martial arts class, think about how people have been doing these movements for thousands of years!

 © Shell Education

Name: ______________________________ Date: ______________

Directions: Read "A Brief History of Martial Arts." Then, answer the questions.

1. What evidence supports the fact that martial arts have been around for centuries?
   - (A) weapons and techniques
   - (B) fingerprints and testimony
   - (C) paintings and documents
   - (D) records and recordings

2. How were martial arts used early on in China?
   - (A) to hunt for food and for combat
   - (B) to train for war and for entertainment
   - (C) to fight with enemies and for personal strength
   - (D) to trick enemies and for learning how to focus

3. How are Japanese martial arts related to samurai?
   - (A) They initially used weapons.
   - (B) They focused on self-defense.
   - (C) They focused on self-improvement.
   - (D) They were only taught to nobility.

4. What is an antonym for *traditional*?
   - (A) classy
   - (B) complicated
   - (C) modern
   - (D) outdated

5. Compare martial arts from China and Japan. You may use facts and details from "Types of Martial Arts" as well.

Martial Arts from China	**Martial Arts from Japan**
Martial Arts from Both Countries	

Name: ______________________ Date: ____________

Directions: Reread "A Brief History of Martial Arts" and the other texts from this week. Then, respond to the prompt.

Compare and contrast two forms of martial arts. Use information and examples from the texts to support your ideas.

______________________ ______________________

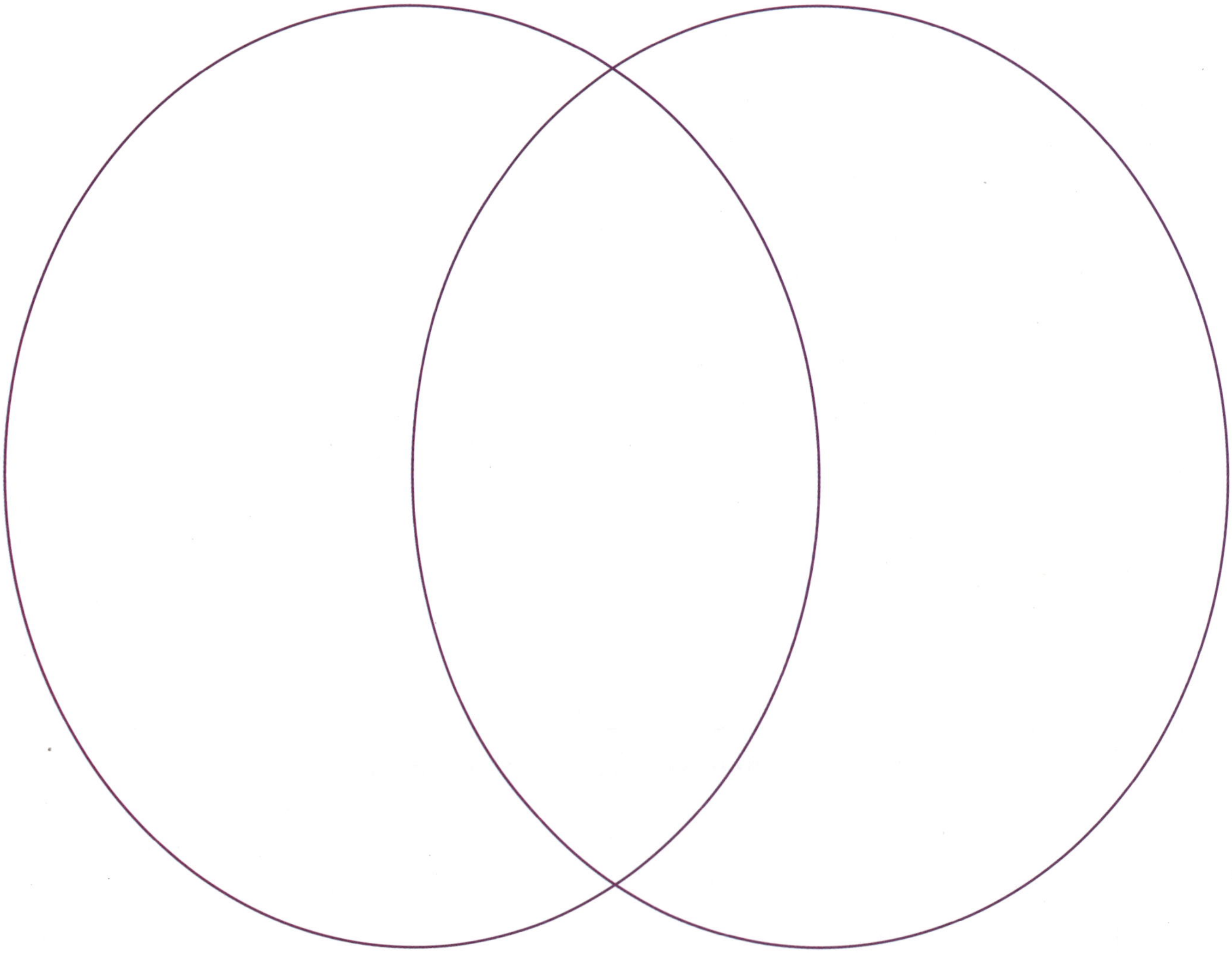

 © Shell Education

Name: ______________________________ Date: ______________

Directions: Read the text, and answer the questions.

As You Read

Make notes in the margins of connections you can make to the text.

Matt's Birthday Present

Matt loved watching martial arts movies. He had always been interested in learning a martial art. It looked like fun, and he wanted to be able to do the things he saw in movies. So when his parents asked him what he wanted for his birthday, Matt immediately knew his answer. He wanted to learn karate!

Matt's mom and dad promised to arrange for him to take lessons. They looked at a few karate studios before they found the right one. They wanted to be sure that the lessons would be safe for Matt. They also wanted to find a lesson schedule that would work for them. Finally, they found what they wanted. Matt was beyond excited. He couldn't wait to start doing what he saw in movies!

1. Why does Matt want karate lessons?
   - (A) His friends take karate lessons.
   - (B) His parents take karate lessons.
   - (C) His teacher suggests he take lessons.
   - (D) He wants to do what he sees in movies.

2. What is karate?
   - (A) a kind of game
   - (B) a kind of home
   - (C) a kind of movie
   - (D) a kind of martial art

3. How do Matt's parents feel about him taking karate lessons?
   - (A) They can't decide.
   - (B) They like the idea.
   - (C) They argue about it.
   - (D) They think karate is too dangerous.

4. What does the phrase *work for them* mean in this text?
   - (A) start a job
   - (B) work hard
   - (C) be agreeable
   - (D) have employees

Name: ______________________ Date: ______________

Directions: Read the text, and answer the questions.

As You Read

Circle words or phrases that describe how characters are feeling.

Matt's First Karate Lesson

Matt was excited to start karate lessons. His parents had gotten him a gi (gee), a white uniform that he would wear when he was practicing. On the first day of his lessons, Matt proudly put his uniform on and joined the other students in his class. Walter, their sensei (sen-SEY), began the class.

But to Matt's dismay, Walter didn't start by teaching the class what Matt had seen in movies. Instead, Walter taught the class how to properly stretch their bodies. Then, he taught them some basic movement exercises. He also taught the class some breathing exercises. He told everyone, "Karate isn't about kicking people or hitting them, and it's not about breaking boards. It's about a person's mind and body working together. It's about self-control."

Matt wasn't sure he liked the sound of that. He didn't know what Walter meant, and he wanted to know when they would get to learn some spinning jump moves. But after all, this was only the first lesson. He was sure he had a lot more to learn.

1. Which simile best describes a *gi*?
   - (A) soft as a feather
   - (B) as tough as nails
   - (C) as white as snow
   - (D) as busy as a bee

2. What is another word for *dismay*?
   - (A) caring
   - (B) disappointment
   - (C) excitement
   - (D) helpfulness

3. What confuses Matt?
   - (A) how to wear a gi
   - (B) how to address his sensei
   - (C) how to follow the movements
   - (D) how the mind and body work together

4. Which of the following words uses the prefix *uni–* similar to how it is used in *uniform*?
   - (A) unicorn
   - (B) uninstall
   - (C) union
   - (D) uninvited

© Shell Education

Name: ______________________________ Date: ______________

Directions: Read the text, and answer the questions.

As You Read

Make notes in the margins of connections you can make to the text.

Matt Learns Karate

Matt found out that karate lessons were very different from what he was used to seeing in movies. The students hadn't done any jumps, kicks, or hits. Instead, they practiced movements. They did their breathing exercises.

Walter told the class that once they had learned the basic karate techniques, they would be able to practice them with one another. At first, Matt was annoyed that he wouldn't be able to practice kicking someone across the room. But he found that even the basic movements they were learning could be difficult. It was seeming like karate was harder than it looked in movies.

Every lesson, Matt learned something new. He worked very hard and was exhausted by the end of his lessons. He always slept very well after a tough lesson.

1. How would Matt describe his karate lessons?
   - (A) boring
   - (B) challenging
   - (C) confusing
   - (D) easy

2. What is another word for *basic*?
   - (A) advanced
   - (B) colorful
   - (C) complex
   - (D) simple

3. Compare Matt's ideas about karate before taking lessons to his understanding after taking lessons.

____

____

4. Explain why you would or would not stick with something even though it fell short of your expectations?

____

____

© Shell Education

Name: ______________________________ Date: ______________

As You Read

Make notes in the margins of connections you can make to the characters or events in text.

Matt's Real Lesson

Matt continued taking his karate lessons. So far, he was no closer to being able to do the things he saw people doing in martial-arts movies. But when he realized that karate just isn't like the movies, he came to enjoy it. Karate made him feel strong and gave him energy, and it also made him feel calm. He found himself looking forward to going to his lessons after school. He kept working hard, and one day, Walter told Matt that he was ready for his first test.

Two weeks before the testing date, Walter gave Matt an application for Matt to take home and fill out. Matt brought it back to the next class. And for the next two weeks, Matt practiced at home every night, while also practicing extra hard at his lessons. He wanted to be sure that he was ready for the test.

On the day of Matt's test, he joined a group of other students who were also ready to take the test. The test began with some exercises. The students had to show that they could do all the movements that Walter had taught them. Then, they had to take a written test. Walter had also taught them some history and concepts of karate, and they had to show that they knew those things, too.

Matt thought he did best at the physical test. Written tests were not really his strong point. When he finished his written test, he handed it in to Walter. He joined the rest of the students and anxiously waited for the results.

After everyone had finished testing, Walter congratulated them on their strong efforts, and then he called up each student to speak to them individually. When it was Matt's turn, Walter told him that he had passed! Matt was over the moon, and he felt happy that all his hard work had paid off. Walter also told Matt that he would receive his first belt, which would be white with a black stripe on it, at the next class.

As Matt went home from karate that night, he thought back on his experiences so far. Karate had turned out to be very different from what he thought it would be, but for that, he was grateful. Most importantly, he had discovered that he liked it very much!

 © Shell Education

Name: ______________________________ Date: ______________

Directions: Read "Matt's Real Lesson." Then, answer the questions.

1. What does Matt think about karate at first?

- (A) It will not be fun.
- (B) It will be extremely easy.
- (C) It will be just like the movies.
- (D) It will be very different from the movies.

2. How do Walter and Matt feel about Matt passing his test?

- (A) pleased
- (B) jealous
- (C) surprised
- (D) frightened

3. What do you predict Matt will do next?

- (A) He will get a new gi.
- (B) He will change karate instructors.
- (C) He will continue taking karate classes.
- (D) He will stop taking karate classes.

4. What lesson does Matt learn?

- (A) Give up when things get too tough.
- (B) Put your own needs first, then think of others.
- (C) Quit when you aren't happy doing something.
- (D) Give new things a try, and you can learn something new.

5. Write three important events in the order in which they occur in the text.

1.	Matt starts karate lessons to learn to do the things he sees people do in martial-arts movies.
2.	
3.	
4.	

Name: ______________________________ Date: ______________

Directions: Reread "Matt's First Karate Lesson" and "Matt's Real Lesson." Then, respond to the prompt.

Write a story about a time you and a friend take karate lessons together. Use descriptive words and phrases and sensory details to tell your story.

© Shell Education

Name: ______________________________ Date: ________________

Karate Class Advertisement Radio Script

Adult's voice: Have you ever wanted to learn how to fight or learn self-defense? Or maybe you'd like a fun place to spend time with friends after school?

Two kids' voices together: We love it here!

Adult's voice: Take it from them, and look no further than Matt's Martial Arts House! We have a variety of martial arts classes. There's something for everyone! We offer Tae kwon do, karate, jujitsu, and more. Call us and ask if we offer what you're looking for! We employ 10 professional martial arts instructors, which allows us to offer a wide range of classes. We have before-school programs, after-school programs, and weekend-only classes. Stop by to take your first class free, and start your martial arts journey today!

Name: ______________________ Date: ____________

Directions: Read "Karate Class Advertisement Radio Script." Then, answer the questions.

1. What is the ad advertising?
   - (A) jujitsu classes
   - (B) after-school classes
   - (C) martial arts classes
   - (D) Tae kwon do classes

2. How do the kids' voices affect the ad?
   - (A) They are meant to distract the listener.
   - (B) They are meant to make the listener excited.
   - (C) They are meant to prove the classes are real.
   - (D) They are meant to make the announcer laugh.

3. What is the purpose of the ad?
   - (A) to inform people of a new business
   - (B) to instruct people of different forms of martial arts
   - (C) to convince people that learning martial arts is important
   - (D) to persuade people to take classes at Matt's Martial Arts House

4. Why does the ad refer to the classes as a *martial arts journey*?
   - (A) One class is not enough to master martial arts.
   - (B) Instructors travel from all over the world to give classes.
   - (C) People who take the classes walk a mile or more to warm up.
   - (D) The classes go on field trips to watch martial arts competitions.

5. Explain why the ad does or does not motivate you to want to sign up for martial arts classes at Matt's Martial Arts House.

____

____

____

____

____

© Shell Education

Name: ______________________________ Date: ________________

Directions: Closely read these texts. Write to explain which martial art you would like to try and why. Draw a picture of you practicing this art.

Close-Reading Texts

Types of Martial Arts	A Brief History of Martial Arts
Karate is also a close combat form of martial art. In karate, striking is mostly used. Striking includes punching, kicking, knee strikes, and elbow strikes. Tae kwon do originated in Korea. It also uses punching and kicking, but Tae kwon do focuses on kicking more than karate does. Kung fu is a general word that refers to Chinese martial arts. There are many types of kung fu, such as Shaolin and tai chi.	Over time, many different styles developed. This includes some styles that don't use weapons. Jujitsu is one of these styles. Today, Japanese martial arts tend to fall into two categories. The first category refers to martial art styles that were created before 1868. These styles are traditional. Their primary use was for war. The second category refers to styles that were created after 1868. These styles are modern. They are often used for self-improvement. Some people may use them for self-defense.

____

____

____

____

____

____

____

____

____

____

____

Name: ______________________ Date: ______________

Directions: Closely read these texts. Compare the people who practice martial arts.

Close-Reading Texts

Matt Learns Karate	A Brief History of Martial Arts
Matt soon found out that real karate lessons were very different from the types of things he was used to seeing in movies. The students hadn't done any jumps, kicks, or hits. Instead, they practiced movements. They did their breathing exercises. Walter told the class that once they had learned the basic karate techniques, they would be able to practice them with one another. At first, Matt was annoyed that he wouldn't be able to practice kicking someone across the room. But he found that even the basic movements they were learning could be difficult.	There are different types of martial arts in Japan. In this country, martial arts started with the samurai. Samurai were important members of the military. They had special privileges. And they were the only members of society that were allowed to use weapons. Because martial arts started with samurai, early Japanese martial arts focused on using weapons in their practices. Over time, many different styles developed. This includes some styles that don't use weapons.

Matt	Samurai

Both

 © Shell Education

Name: ______________________ Date: ______________

Directions: Think about the texts in this unit. Then, respond to the prompt.

Matt's Sensei explained that martial arts are "about mind and body working together." What does this mean? Explain this idea, then describe how it could be used in another activity. Use precise language and vocabulary to develop your ideas.

Name: ______________________ Date: ______________

Directions: You play a sport that you are very excited about. Write a radio ad to persuade others to sign up. Use dialogue similar to the radio ad on page 185. Include a persuasive technique such as repetition, a celebrity endorsement, or an appeal to others' emotions.

© Shell Education

Name: ______________________________ Date: ______________

Directions: Read the text, and answer the questions.

As You Read

Place a star beside new or interesting facts.
Underline facts you knew before reading.

Busy Sleeping

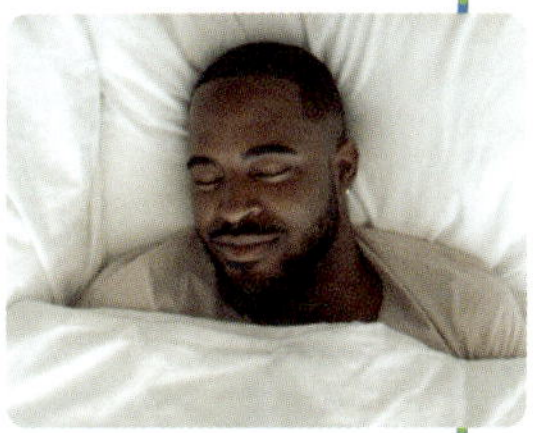

When you go to sleep at night, you probably think that you are not doing anything. Your body stays on your bed, your eyes are closed, and you don't talk to people. But there is a lot of activity happening inside your body while you are asleep! Scientists have used special, sophisticated machines to study what happens when people go to sleep. They have found that people's brains are very busy when they sleep. Every night, a person's brain goes through a sleep cycle multiple times. There are several stages of sleep in one of these cycles. Brain activity level is a little different in each stage. The last stage of the cycle is called rapid eye movement, or REM, sleep. During REM, a person's eyes move even though they are asleep. That is how this stage got its name. Most people's dreams occur during REM sleep.

1. What is true about a person's brain while they are sleeping?
   - (A) It is very busy.
   - (B) It is also asleep.
   - (C) It is able to rest.
   - (D) It is unable to work.

2. What happens to people during REM sleep?
   - (A) They are awake.
   - (B) They feel sick.
   - (C) They talk a lot.
   - (D) They dream.

3. What does *sophisticated* mean?
   - (A) complex
   - (B) fast
   - (C) slow
   - (D) unique

4. What is meant by a *sleep cycle*?
   - (A) riding a bicycle while sleeping
   - (B) rolling around in bed while sleeping
   - (C) stages of sleep that repeat over and over
   - (D) steps people go through before going to bed

© Shell Education

Name: ______________________________ Date: ________________

Directions: Read the text, and answer the questions.

As You Read

Underline reasons scientists think people dream.

The Importance of Dreams

Do you ever remember your dreams? Even though you may not remember what you dream, research has shown that you probably dream every night. Scientists are not entirely sure why people have dreams. Some scientists believe it is the brain's way of processing things. People learn a lot and experience a lot of things during the day. So, some scientists think that dreaming might be the way a person's brain makes sense of what happens to them. Other scientists say that dreams are the way people's brains solve problems. For example, if someone is upset about something, dreams may be a way for their brain to help them feel better.

Scientists may not agree on why people dream. But they do agree that dreaming is very important. People need to dream so that their brains are ready for the next day.

1. Based on the text, what can you infer about dreams?
   - (A) People must dream to survive.
   - (B) People use dreams to make up stories.
   - (C) People write about dreams in personal journals.
   - (D) People have studied dreams for a long time.

2. What do we *process* similar to how we process information?
   - (A) paper
   - (B) people
   - (C) potatoes
   - (D) problems

3. What is one main idea of the text?
   - (A) Falling asleep quickly helps people dream better.
   - (B) People who sleep in a bed have good dreams.
   - (C) People need at least eight hours of sleep.
   - (D) Dreaming is important for our brains.

4. Which word uses the prefix *dis-* similar to its meaning in *disagree*?
   - (A) discuss
   - (B) disco
   - (C) dishonest
   - (D) distance

 © Shell Education

Name: ______________________ Date: ____________

Directions: Read the text, and answer the questions.

As You Read

Underline reasons sleep is important to the body, mind, and spirit.

Sleep for Body, Mind, and Spirit

Sleep is a very important part of staying healthy. When people are asleep, their brains use that time to take care of themselves. Some scientists think that people's brains sort things out when they sleep and that they also replace the chemicals they need. And while people are sleeping, their bodies stay busy by using that time to heal themselves. During sleep, people's bodies use that time to build up their immune systems, which is the system used to fight off germs. Younger people's bodies also use sleep time to build up muscles, bones, and tissues so that they can grow. Sleep also helps people think clearly and stay in better moods. That helps them cope better if they have a busy day.

1. Why might people sleep more when they are sick or injured?
   - (A) to catch up on lost sleep
   - (B) so they may continue growing
   - (C) to gain energy for the day's events
   - (D) so their bodies may heal and fight off germs

2. If you *cope with* a busy day, what happens?
   - (A) You fear a lot of work.
   - (B) You avoid a lot of work.
   - (C) You manage a lot of work.
   - (D) You desire a lot of work.

3. How is sleep good for your body? ______________________

____

____

4. Explain why you agree or disagree that "sleep helps people think clearly and stay in better moods."

____

____

Name: ________________________ Date: ______________

As You Read

Place a star beside suggestions for falling asleep you follow now. Place an exclamation point beside suggestions you do not follow but might try.

Sweet Dreams

A good night's sleep is very important for a person's health. People's brains and bodies use that time to do all kinds of things that they cannot do as well when they're awake. People of different ages need different amounts of sleep. Many experts say that children between the ages of 6 and 12 need about 9–12 hours of sleep per night. It is recommended that teenagers get 8–10 hours of sleep. And adults should sleep at least 7 hours per night.

Sometimes, it's not easy to get the sleep that you need. You might have a hard time falling asleep because you have a lot of energy or excitement and don't feel tired. Maybe you're worried about something, and you can't seem to slow your thoughts down. When these things happen, it's hard to get sleepy. So, here are some things to keep in mind to make it easier for you to get the sleep you need:

- Keep your body in a routine by going to bed at the same time every night.
- Do something calming right before bedtime, such as taking a warm bath or reading.
- Limit sodas, iced tea, and other foods and drinks that contain caffeine, which can keep you awake.
- Turn off your TV when it is time to sleep. Better yet, don't have a TV in your room. Studies show that children who have a TV in their rooms sleep less.
- Don't watch scary TV shows or movies close to bedtime because these can make it hard to fall asleep.
- Exercise during the day because it will help you sleep better at night. But don't exercise just before going to bed because it could keep you awake.
- Don't do homework, play games, or talk on the phone in bed. If you use your bed just for sleeping, you'll train your body to associate your bed with sleep.

If you follow these handy tips, you will develop some healthy sleeping habits. These will make it easier for you to be more relaxed before bedtime so you can fall asleep and stay asleep.

 © Shell Education

Name: ______________________________ Date: ________________

Directions: Read "Sweet Dreams." Then, answer the questions.

1. Why might the author have used a bulleted list?
   - (A) to use less space on the page
   - (B) to organize events in chronological order
   - (C) to list details according to their importance
   - (D) to focus the reader's attention on key details

2. Which of the following is one main idea of this text?
   - (A) Use your bed just for sleeping.
   - (B) You might have a lot of energy.
   - (C) Try to go to bed at the same time every night.
   - (D) A good night's sleep is very important for your health.

3. What can you infer about caffeine?
   - (A) It is hard to find.
   - (B) It can keep you awake.
   - (C) It can make you sleepy.
   - (D) It is good for your health.

4. Which idea from "Sleep for Body, Mind, and Spirit" is also shared in "Sweet Dreams"?
   - (A) Sleep helps you think clearly.
   - (B) Your entire body needs sleep.
   - (C) Sleep is a very important part of staying healthy.
   - (D) The brain replaces the chemicals it needs when you sleep.

5. List three details from the text that support the main idea.

Main Idea You can do several things to help yourself fall asleep at night.

Name: ____________________ Date: ______________

Directions: Reread "Sweet Dreams" and the earlier texts from this week. Then, respond to the prompt.

A friend does not get enough sleep. They are cranky and lack energy during the day. Write a letter to explain to your friend why they should get more sleep and how to sleep better. Support your reasons with facts and details from at least one text.

© Shell Education

Name: ______________________________ Date: ______________

Directions: Read the text, and answer the questions.

As You Read

Underline Isaac's problem. Place stars beside what he does to try to solve the problem.

Isaac the House Cat

Isaac was a house cat. His favorite activities included chasing his toy mice, sunbathing, and getting into boxes. He especially enjoyed sitting in high places. But most of all, his favorite activity was sleeping. He couldn't get enough of it.

Or at least, he used to. Isaac was having some serious sleep issues lately, and they were causing him to feel grumpy and tired. He wasn't his energetic self anymore. He hadn't been for a few weeks, ever since his owners had moved into a new house.

Isaac had tried everything to get a good night's sleep. He spent hours laying in the sun every day, but all it did was make his fur feel warm. At the old house, laying in the sun would put him right to sleep. Then, he thought climbing the tower and laying in the soft basket at the top would do the trick. But nothing he tried seemed to work, and Isaac let out a howl of frustration.

1. What is Isaac's problem?
   - Ⓐ He cannot find a place to sunbathe.
   - Ⓑ He has very itchy skin.
   - Ⓒ He does not like the tower.
   - Ⓓ He is having trouble sleeping.

2. What is another word for an *issue*?
   - Ⓐ agreement
   - Ⓑ concern
   - Ⓒ solution
   - Ⓓ topic

3. How does Isaac try to solve his issue?
   - Ⓐ He tries to take longer naps.
   - Ⓑ He watches the birds outside.
   - Ⓒ He runs around and plays.
   - Ⓓ He spends time in the sunspot.

4. What is a synonym for a *solution*?
   - Ⓐ answer
   - Ⓑ discussion
   - Ⓒ problem
   - Ⓓ question

Name: ______________________________ Date: ______________

Directions: Read the text, and answer the questions.

As You Read

Circle words that are new or interesting.

Isaac Visits the Doctor

Hallie was super annoyed that her cat, Isaac, was constantly waking her up at night. It seemed like Isaac wasn't able to get the restful sleep that he needed.

"I can't keep doing this," Hallie told her mom one morning after she nearly fell asleep over her plate of waffles. "Does Isaac need to go to the doctor?"

Her mom shrugged and looked over at Isaac. Hallie's mom grabbed one of Isaac's toy mice from the tile floor and threw it across the room. But Isaac didn't react to it at all, and he just sat there, blinking slowly at her.

"I guess he does seem lethargic," her mom said.

So after school that day, Hallie and her mom took Isaac to their local vet. Hallie explained the sleeping issues that Isaac seemed to be having and how it seemed like he was depressed and didn't want to play at all like he used to. She hoped the vet would understand and have some answers for her.

1. Why does Hallie think something is wrong with Isaac?
   - (A) Isaac is waking her up at night.
   - (B) Isaac is not eating his food.
   - (C) He keeps running around.
   - (D) He keeps get into boxes.

2. Why does Hallie take Isaac to see the doctor?
   - (A) to be nosy
   - (B) to help him feel better
   - (C) to make him uncomfortable
   - (D) to challenge his claim of not sleeping

3. Which words best describe how Hallie feels about Isaac's situation?
   - (A) *relaxed* and *unconcerned*
   - (B) *angry* and *confused*
   - (C) *excited* and *hopeful*
   - (D) *frustrated* and *worried*

4. What is the meaning of the word *lethargic*?
   - (A) sleepy or lazy
   - (B) full of energy
   - (C) playful
   - (D) strange or unusual

 © Shell Education

Name: ______________________________ Date: ______________

Directions: Read the text, and answer the questions.

As You Read

Circle the likely causes of Isaac's issue.

Isaac's Sleep Habits

Luckily, the veterinarian seemed to understand the problem and how to help.

"Cats are most active at dusk and at dawn," the vet said, examining Isaac. "But I find it odd that he is not sleeping at all during the night."

As the vet examined Isaac, his eyes looked as wide as saucers. The vet gently lifted his paws and poked his twitching tail.

"Have you made any changes lately to his regular routine?" the vet asked them.

Hallie's mom gasped softly, and Hallie looked up at her in surprise.

"Of course! We recently moved into a new house," Hallie's mom said. The vet nodded and talked about how cats could be sensitive to stress, which can result in sleep issues. She gave them some tips, including buying new food, more playtime, and setting up more scratching and hiding areas.

It was Hallie's turn to be stressed, but she was hopeful the vet's tips would help Isaac adjust to the new house.

1. What is likely the cause of Isaac's sleeping issues?
   - (A) He is stressed from moving.
   - (B) The weather has been cold.
   - (C) He is nervous about the vet.
   - (D) He does not have anywhere comfy to sleep.

2. What is the phrase *his eyes looked as wide as saucers* and example of?
   - (A) alliteration
   - (B) hyperbole
   - (C) onomatopoeia
   - (D) simile

3. How does Hallie feel the end of the text? Why does she feel that way?

   ____

4. Why do you think a hiding place might help Isaac? ______________________

   ____

Name: ______________________ Date: ____________

As You Read

Underline important events in the story.

Time to Sleep

Isaac dashed out of his carrier when Hallie set him down in the living room, ran to the middle cubby in the tower, and curled up, hoping he wouldn't have to go to the vet ever again. The vet was honestly the worst!

Hallie came over to the tower with Isaac's food bowl. Isaac's stomach growled, but when he smelled the food that Hallie set down, he recoiled from it.

Isaac let out a long meow. Frankly, he was tired of everything new! He didn't like the new smells or the new rooms in the new house, and now there was new food. When he finally fell asleep, he had a terrible nightmare that he was being chased by an evil toy mouse. He was terrified when he woke up, so he ran to Hallie's room. He dove under the covers with her and stayed there until morning.

The next day, Isaac was feeling a little bit better. He didn't want to be near the new food again, but Hallie was trying so hard to get him to eat it. He felt obligated to give it a try. He was surprised to find that he liked the salmon.

Then, Isaac took a nice nap. When he woke up, Hallie was sitting next to him on the couch and had gathered a bunch of his toy mice.

"Here Isaac," she called to him, walking away and waving the mouse. Isaac had to follow her, of course—he could tell she was trying to play with him. And then Hallie tossed it into a room Isaac had not explored yet. He was hesitant to go inside the room, and he did so cautiously.

For the rest of the afternoon, Hallie and Isaac played with the toy mice. A few hours later, he had seen every room in the new house, and it wasn't as bad as he thought. Plus, he forgot how exhilarating it was to chase toy mice.

After they played, Hallie created a new scratch post by cutting up a bunch of cardboard boxes and tying them together. He tried scratching the new post and found it extremely soothing. Plus, when Isaac was done scratching, he realized Hallie had also created a soft hiding place for him. She coaxed him into a cardboard box filled with blankets that made him feel like he was floating on cloud. He burrowed deep inside them so he couldn't see any afternoon light and fell asleep.

At dinner time, Isaac wolfed down his salmon and then settled into Hallie's lap for an evening cuddle. The best thing about the day was that even though Isaac had taken several naps, he was still very tired at bedtime and was fast asleep in no time!

© Shell Education

Name: ______________________________ Date: ________________

Directions: Read "Time to Sleep." Then, answer the questions.

1. What does the phrase *he recoiled from it* tell readers about Isaac's feelings toward the new food?

- (A) He is too full to eat any more food.
- (B) He is confused and does not think it is for him.
- (C) He is hungry and excited to try something new.
- (D) He is not interested in trying it.

2. What is the result of trying the tips from the vet?

- (A) Isaac is tired and does not want to play.
- (B) Isaac is able to sleep better at night.
- (C) Isaac is able to jump higher.
- (D) Isaac is hungry but eats less food.

3. If something is *soothing*, what does that mean?

- (A) It has a calming effect.
- (B) It makes a loud noise.
- (C) It vibrates quickly.
- (D) It exerts a strong force.

4. Which word is a synonym for *exhilarating*?

- (A) frustrating
- (B) confusing
- (C) exhausting
- (D) exciting

5. Record four important events in the order in which they occurred.

1.	
2.	
3.	
4.	
5.	Isaac is able to fall asleep and stay asleep through the night.

Name: ______________________ Date: ____________

Directions: Reread "Time to Sleep." Then, respond to the prompt.

Describe a dream you have had recently. Explain how it made you feel when you woke up.

© Shell Education

Name: ______________________________ Date: ________________

A Limerick on Sleep

There once was a boy who liked sleeping.
In his dreams, he liked to go leaping.
At night, his dog would come snuggle,
But this made sleeping a struggle.
No worries, he had some tea steeping!

Name: ______________________________ Date: ______________

Directions: Read "A Limerick on Sleep." Then, answer the questions.

1. What does the boy like to do?
   - (A) eat
   - (B) drink tea
   - (C) play with his dog
   - (D) sleep

2. What are the boy's dreams about?
   - (A) eating
   - (B) drinking tea
   - (C) leaping
   - (D) playing with his dog

3. How does the boy's dog affect him?
   - (A) It interrupts his slumber.
   - (B) It shows up in his dreams.
   - (C) It provides warmth on cold nights.
   - (D) It jumps on him at night.

4. What is another word for *steeping*?
   - (A) breaking
   - (B) cooling
   - (C) soaking
   - (D) warming

5. What do you do when you have trouble sleeping? Does this help you fall asleep?

____

____

____

____

____

 © Shell Education

Name: ______________________________ Date: ________________

Directions: Closely read these texts. List four facts you learn about sleep.

Close-Reading Texts

Busy Sleeping	Isaac's Sleep Habits
When you go to sleep at night, you probably think that you are not doing anything. Your body stays on your bed, your eyes are closed, and you don't talk to people. But there is a lot of activity happening inside your body while you are asleep! Scientists have used special, sophisticated machines to study what happens when people go to sleep. They have found that people's brains are very busy when they sleep. Every night, a person's brain goes through a sleep cycle multiple times.	"Of course! We recently moved into a new house," Hallie's mom said. The vet nodded and talked about how cats could be sensitive to stress, which can result in sleep issues. She gave them some tips, including buying new food, more playtime, and setting up more scratching and hiding areas.

Facts about Sleep

1. ____

____

2. ____

____

3. ____

____

4. ____

____

© Shell Education

Name: ______________________________ Date: ______________

Directions: Closely read these texts. Identify and compare and contrast the structure of each text.

Close-Reading Texts

Sweet Dreams	Isaac the House Cat
Here are some things you can do to make it easier for you to get the sleep you need: • Keep your body in a routine by going to bed at the same time every night. • Do something calming right before bedtime, such as taking a warm bath or reading. • Limit sodas, iced tea, and other foods and drinks that contain caffeine. • Exercise during the day—it will help you sleep better at night. But don't exercise just before going to bed.	Isaac was having some serious sleep issues lately, and they were causing him to feel grumpy and tired. He wasn't his energetic self anymore. He hadn't been for a few weeks, ever since his owners had moved into a new house. Isaac had tried everything to get a good night's sleep. He spent hours laying in the sun every day, but all it did was make his fur feel warm. At the old house, laying in the sun would put him right to sleep. Then, he thought climbing the tower and laying in the soft basket at the top would do the trick.

Text Structures

cause-effect

chronological order

compare-contrast

promblem-solution

Text	Text Structure	How You Know
Sweet Dreams		
Isaac the House Cat		

© Shell Education

Name: ______________________________ Date: ________________

Directions: Think about the texts from this unit. Then, respond to the prompt.

Some people keep a "sleep diary" to monitor their sleep. It helps them find patterns in their behavior that may affect their sleep. Complete this sleep diary for several nights. Write the date. Write what you did before going to sleep. Then, rate your sleep the next morning.

Sleep Rating

1—terrible 2—not too good 3—okay 4—pretty good 5—fantastic!

Date	What I Did Before Bed	Sleep Rating

© Shell Education

Name: ________________________________ Date: ________________

Directions: Write a poem about sleeping. Make sure your poem has a rhyme pattern. If you want, learn about limericks, and write a limerick. Illustrate your poem.

© Shell Education

Name: ______________________ Date: ____________

Directions: Read the text, and answer the questions.

As You Read

Underline information that is new to you. Put a star beside information you knew before reading.

All about Go-Karts

Have you ever imagined what it would be like to drive a race car, speeding down the road like a flash of lightning? If you have, you can learn how to race go-karts! Go-kart racing is sometimes called *karting*. People who participate in this sport learn how to drive go-karts, which look a lot like race cars. They race around a track, competing with one another to see who can be the fastest driver, similar to other auto races. Some amusement parks have outdoor go-kart racing tracks. And some companies have created indoor go-kart racing tracks in large buildings.

There are different types of go-karts. Some go-karts are made for children or for people who are new to the sport. They don't go very fast, but they are good go-karts to use for beginners. Other go-karts go very fast. Some people who want to become professional race car drivers use those.

1. What are go-karts?
   - (A) special bicycles
   - (B) special boats
   - (C) special cars
   - (D) special trucks

2. The phrase *auto races* in the text is short for *automobile races*. What is the meaning of *automobile*?
   - (A) a car you drive yourself
   - (B) a movement you make
   - (C) moving from one place to another by itself
   - (D) something that hangs by itself

3. Why might people drive go-karts?
   - (A) to run errands
   - (B) to learn to drive
   - (C) to transport heavy objects
   - (D) to take someone to the airport

4. What is the meaning of the phrase *like a flash of lightning*?
   - (A) really bright
   - (B) really fast
   - (C) really loud
   - (D) really scary

Name: ______________________ Date: ____________

Directions: Read the text, and answer the questions.

As You Read

Number each of the safety tips the author suggests.

Go-Kart Safety

Go-karting can be a lot of fun, but it can be dangerous, too. People should always make sure to wear helmets and safety glasses when they are riding go-karts. They should also check to be sure that their clothes and hair cannot catch on any of the moving parts. Before people get into go-karts, workers usually check to make sure that each go-kart is working properly. People should not ride any go-karts that are making weird noises or not running well.

People should also follow safety rules once they are using go-karts. Staying in the go-kart seat at all times is important. They should never try to get out of the seat when the go-kart is moving. They should keep their go-kart on the track and watch their speed. Following these precautions will help them have a safe and fun ride.

1. Why does the author give safety tips about go-karting?
   - (A) Go-karting can be fun.
   - (B) Go-karting can be dangerous.
   - (C) Go-karting can be a sport.
   - (D) Go-karting can be time-consuming.

2. Why does the author suggest being sure that clothes and hair cannot catch on moving parts?
   - (A) to avoid being injured
   - (B) to avoid going too fast
   - (C) to avoid going off the track
   - (D) to avoid stopping too quickly

3. What is another word for *unusual*?
   - (A) challenging
   - (B) expensive
   - (C) secret
   - (D) strange

4. What is the meaning of *precautions*?
   - (A) actions taken ahead of time to avoid danger
   - (B) actions taken after doing something dangerous
   - (C) actions taken while doing something dangerous
   - (D) actions taken while doing something safe

© Shell Education

Name: ______________________________ Date: ______________

Directions: Read the text, and answer the questions.

As You Read

Circle the words that identify parts of a go-kart.

Go-Kart Construction

Go-karts consist of several basic parts. The largest and most visible part of a go-kart is the frame, which can be painted in a variety of ways. Attached to the frame is the driver's seat. Some go-karts are built for just one person and have one seat, while other go-karts have room for two seats. Go-karts also have engines. Some engines are very powerful, and some engines are not. The engine's power depends on the type of go-kart. Expert drivers tend to use go-karts that have more powerful engines than the go-karts that children use. Each go-kart engine is connected to a special device called the *transmission*. Of course, a go-kart wouldn't get very far without wheels, so each go-kart has four tires, too.

1. Which is connected to a go-kart's engine?
   - (A) frame
   - (B) steering wheel
   - (C) transmission
   - (D) wheels

2. Which word is defined as the body of a go-kart?
   - (A) device
   - (B) frame
   - (C) steering wheel
   - (D) transmission

3. Why are children's go-kart engines not as powerful as experts' go-kart engines?

____

____

4. How difficult do you think it is to build a go-kart? Explain your thinking.

____

____

____

Name: ______________________ Date: ______________

As You Read

Underline the different types of go-kart races. Circle facts about them.

In the Driver's Seat

Go-karting is a very popular sport in the United States. It's popular in many other countries, too. Children as young as seven or eight years old can start racing. In the United States, there are even special "kid karts" for children as young as five. There are many indoor and outdoor go-kart tracks and raceways. Some amusement parks even have go-kart tracks. Sometimes, people practice on them for fun, and other times, races are held.

There are three kinds of go-kart races, and the first type is sprint races. These are very short races. Usually, the track for a sprint race forms an oval that is between 0.25–1 miles (0.4–1.6 kilometers) long. Most of these sprint races last about 15 minutes or less. The most important thing that a person needs to win a sprint race is speed. The faster their go-kart can safely go, the more likely they are to win.

Endurance races are the second kind of go-kart races. These are longer than sprint races, and they typically last from 30 to 45 minutes. Some endurance races last even longer than that. To win an endurance race, a person needs a very well-made go-kart that will smoothly drive for a longer period of time. The person also needs to keep their speed even over the whole distance.

Speedway races are the last type of go-kart races. They take place on special tracks that are even smaller than sprint race tracks. In speedway racing, drivers do several laps around the track.

Whatever kind of go-kart racing a person chooses, go-karting can be a lot of fun. Almost anybody can do it because they don't have to be very big or strong. Are you interested in learning to drive a go-kart? There are many places where you can learn. Lots of cities and towns have go-karting schools, teachers, and lessons. You might find you really enjoy being in the driver's seat!

© Shell Education

Name: ______________________ Date: ______________

Directions: Read "In the Driver's Seat." Then, answer the questions.

1. Which detail supports this main idea: There are three kinds of go kart races.
   - (A) Go-karting is very popular.
   - (B) Some amusement parks have go-kart tracks.
   - (C) Endurance races are different from sprint races.
   - (D) Lots of cities have go-karting schools, teachers, and lessons.

2. What can you infer about kid karts as they compare to regular go-karts?
   - (A) Kid karts go much faster.
   - (B) The karts are the same size.
   - (C) Kid karts are bigger than go-karts.
   - (D) Kid karts are smaller than go-karts.

3. What do endurance racers want?
   - (A) expensive karts
   - (B) karts that will last for a long time
   - (C) karts that will go very fast for a short time
   - (D) karts that will go very fast and then very slowly

4. Which best summarizes this text?
   - (A) Go-karting is very dangerous.
   - (B) Go-karting requires a lot of practice.
   - (C) Go-karting is not fun for most people.
   - (D) Go-karting is very popular and exciting.

5. Compare and contrast sprint races and endurance races using facts and details from the text.

Sprint Races	Endurance Races
Both	

Name: ______________________________ Date: ______________

Directions: Reread "All about Go-Karts" and "In the Driver's Seat." Then, respond to the prompt.

Write to explain why go-karting is or is not a good sport to participate in. Provide logically ordered reasons and support them with facts and details.

© Shell Education

Name: ______________________ Date: ______________

Directions: Read the text, and answer the questions.

As You Read

Circle words that indicate a time-order relationship.

Need for Speed

Hank loved to go fast. He would challenge anyone at recess to a running race, even the older kids, and he always won! Hank's father also loved speed, so much so that he made a career out of it. Hank's dad was a professional race car driver, and he was one of the best. Hank wanted to be just like his father, and he dreamed of the day when he could finally maneuver a car around the tracks.

One day, his father took him to watch a go-kart race. He told Hank he could try driving and racing go-karts until he was old enough to race real race cars. Hank got so excited that he almost started to feel dizzy. Immediately after the race, Hank's dad took him to ride a go-kart for the first time. As soon as Hank settled into his go-kart, he knew he had found his passion in life.

1. How are Hank and his father alike?
   - (A) They both drive cars.
   - (B) They both own go-karts.
   - (C) They both like challenges.
   - (D) They both have a passion for speed.

2. What is a *professional* race car driver?
   - (A) Someone who owns fast cars.
   - (B) Someone who wins every race.
   - (C) Someone who races cars for a living.
   - (D) Someone who teaches others to race.

3. Which event happens first?
   - (A) Hank gets a go-kart.
   - (B) Hank drives a go-kart.
   - (C) Hank goes to a go-kart race.
   - (D) Hank finds his life's passion.

4. What is the meaning of *maneuver*?
   - (A) fix
   - (B) focus
   - (C) operate
   - (D) speed

Name: ______________________________ Date: ______________

Directions: Read the text, and answer the questions.

As You Read

Make notes of connections you can make to the characters or events in the story.

A Slower Pace

Timmy had started fifth grade as a new student at Hank's school. Timmy and Hank became great friends. Like Hank, Timmy also enjoyed racing, but he could never quite run as fast as Hank. Timmy would race Hank at recess, but he would always lose. Hank was nice about winning and he encouraged Timmy to keep practicing, so Timmy kept dreaming of winning a race one day.

One day, Hank ran up to Timmy and was out of breath from excitement.

"You've got to come go-karting with me," Hank told Timmy. "We can race!"

Timmy had never heard of go-karting, but once Hank explained what it was, he couldn't wait to tell his parents about it.

"Go-karting?" Timmy's mom asked him. "Isn't that a little dangerous?"

Timmy shrugged, remembering that Hank hadn't said anything at all about danger. Timmy wondered how he could convince his mom to let him try it.

1. How are Timmy and Hank alike?
   - Ⓐ They both are fast.
   - Ⓑ They both like to race.
   - Ⓒ They both have go-karts.
   - Ⓓ They both race to school.

2. Why do Timmy's parents question Hank's idea?
   - Ⓐ They worry that Timmy will not like it.
   - Ⓑ They think it is expensive.
   - Ⓒ They don't like Hank.
   - Ⓓ They think it is dangerous.

3. Hank explains that they can *race together*! Why does this sentence end with an exclamation point?
   - Ⓐ The recess field is noisy.
   - Ⓑ Hank is angry at Timmy.
   - Ⓒ Hank is excited.
   - Ⓓ Hank wants to scare Timmy.

4. What does *encouraged* mean?
   - Ⓐ made feel bad
   - Ⓑ gave advice to
   - Ⓒ helped to feel better
   - Ⓓ offered friendship to

© Shell Education

Name: ______________________ Date: ____________

Directions: Read the text, and answer the questions.

As You Read

Circle adjectives that describe characters in the story.

The Go-Kart Compromise

Timmy's dad was also worried about safety. Even after he did some research about the safety gear he would wear, his parents were still unsure. They just didn't want him to get hurt.

Thoughts of go-karting became the only thing Timmy could think about. He even built a fake go-kart out of cardboard in his room and pretended to drive it.

Eventually, his parents noticed how passionate Timmy was. They to put their fears aside and let him try it. But they gave him one condition. He had to be extra careful. So, before they would let Timmy race, they had him take a special go-karting class. They also made him wear extra padding.

"This way, you'll know how to drive a go-kart safely," his mom told him.

Timmy could barely breathe under all his protective layers, but he still gave her a weak thumbs-up.

1. Why does Timmy make and drive a pretend go-kart?
   - (A) He is bored.
   - (B) He wants to fulfill his dream.
   - (C) He likes playing pretend games.
   - (D) He thinks it would turn into a real go-kart.

2. What does *passionate* mean?
   - (A) to be scared or unsure
   - (B) to be confused
   - (C) to feel strongly or excited
   - (D) to be extra safe

3. On what conditions do Timmy's parents allow him to try go-karting?

   ____

4. How do you think Timmy feels after his parents change their minds? Why?

   ____

   ____

© Shell Education

Name: ______________________________ Date: ________________

As You Read

Place a star beside the turning point, or climax, in the story. Underline the outcome.

A Race to Remember

The next day, Timmy approached Hank at recess with a massive smile.

"Hey Hank!" he yelled. "Guess who's going to be go-karting after all?"

"No way—I can't wait to race you!" Hank said, giving Timmy a high five.

The weekend came, and Hank and Timmy met up at the Dome, the most popular go-kart track in their city. After going over the safety rules, they each had a one-on-one lesson with an instructor. Hank's instructor taught him the importance of speed, while Timmy's instructor focused on patience and safety.

"Slow and steady wins the race," Timmy's instructor kept saying.

Alright, alright, I get it already! Timmy wanted to tell him, feeling impatient and anxious as he watched Hank flying by him on the track. But then Timmy thought about his mom's insistence on safety. *Well, even though focusing entirely on speed works for Hank, that doesn't mean that it will work for me*, he thought.

For the next few weekends, Timmy and Hank competed in go-karting races, preparing for an upcoming competition. Every single time, Hank won the race. Timmy felt discouraged, but every loss made him more determined.

Finally, the day of the championship had arrived. Hank and Timmy were lined up, ready, and determined. The racing flag dropped, and off they went!

Timmy was focused. They were on the final lap when Timmy realized he was in the middle of the pack. There were still 10 cars in front of him, and Hank was leading everyone. *Keep it slow and steady*, he thought.

During the final turn, there appeared to be a minor crash! Hank had turned the corner too fast and hit the side of the track. Many of the go-karts behind Hank swerved to avert disaster and had spun out of control. As he drove up to the crash, Timmy was relieved to see Hank put a thumbs-up in the air, indicating no one was injured. As he passed Hank's car, Timmy realized that he was suddenly in first place!

Just when Timmy thought he was in the clear on the final stretch, he looked over to see that Hank was catching up. Timmy pushed the gas pedal to the floor. It was a calculated risk, and he felt it was the right move.

Timmy crossed the finish line a split-second before Hank did! Timmy started to smile, in awe of the fact that he had won the race.

© Shell Education

Name: ______________________ Date: ____________

Directions: Read "A Race to Remember." Then, answer the questions.

1. What is a good moral or lesson for the story?

- (A) Be nice, even when it is hard.
- (B) Confidence always wins over cowardice.
- (C) Give people what they want, and they will be grateful.
- (D) Patience and determination will help you reach your goals.

2. How do the two go-kart instructors compare?

- (A) Timmy's teaches safety, but Hank's teaches speed.
- (B) Timmy's rides with him, but Hank's does not.
- (C) Timmy's wears a helmet, but Hank's does not.
- (D) Timmy's talks a lot, but Hank's is quiet.

3. Which is the best example when "slow and steady wins the race"?

- (A) when washing a car
- (B) when going to sleep
- (C) when playing piano
- (D) when climbing a mountain

4. Which word means the opposite of *discouraged*?

- (A) courageous
- (B) discouraging
- (C) encouraged
- (D) uncourageous

5. Write an effect for each cause.

Cause	Effect
Hank and Timmy need to learn to drive go-karts.	
Hank wins most of the practice races.	
Hank turns a corner too fast in the championship race.	

UNIT 12
WEEK 2
DAY
5

Name: ______________________________ Date: ______________

Directions: Reread "A Race to Remember." Then, respond to the prompt.

Write a story about being in a go-kart race. Use dialogue and descriptive language in your story.

© Shell Education

Go-Kart History

1956

Art Ingels was the "the father of karting." He had a friend who helped him. His friend's name was Lou Borelli. They created the first go-kart. They used scrap metal and a lawn mower engine.

1956

The first time a go-kart was seen in public. This was at the Pomona sports car races in California. After this, homemade go-karts became more popular. Many people started to create their own versions.

1956–1957

Races started popping up in different places. People often chose to race in parking lots because they were large, flat, and open. One of the places they chose to race was the Rose Bowl Stadium in Pasadena, California.

1957

Bill Rowles, Duffy Livingstone, and Roy Desbrow wanted to make a lot of go-karts in a short amount of time. They founded the Go-Kart Manufacturing Company. This allowed people to buy and own go-karts. That made it possible for many people to try out go-karting.

1957

Don Broberick and 12 others formed the Go Kart Club of America (GKCA; now called the International Karting Federation). They created rules and guidelines for everyone to follow.

1957–1958

Ingels and Borelli started a go-kart manufacturing company. It was called *Ingels & Borelli Kart Company*. They called their kart the Caretta.

1959

The first permanent go-kart track was created. It was meant to be a place for testing and competitions. It was located in Azusa, California.

1959

GKCA held the first Grand National go-kart racing event. It was held at the newly constructed track. This made the sport more popular.

1960

Go-karting continued to grow in popularity. It expanded from California to the rest of the United States. And eventually, there were karting events around the world.

1962

Internationally, karting became regulated by an organization called FIA, and an annual Karting World Championship was born.

© Shell Education

Name: ______________________________ Date: ______________

Directions: Read "Go-Kart History." Then, answer the questions.

1. How much time passed between the world's first go-kart and the world's first permanent karting track?
   - (A) 1 month
   - (B) 1 year
   - (C) 3 months
   - (D) 3 years

2. Why are parking lots popular places to race go-karts?
   - (A) They are large, flat, and wide open.
   - (B) People can grab snacks to enjoy the races.
   - (C) They can hold a lot of people in a small area.
   - (D) People can stay safe when the go-karts are racing.

3. What does the author mean by "Races started *popping up* in all different types of places"?
   - (A) The karts made loud popping sounds.
   - (B) There were a lot of races all of a sudden.
   - (C) People at the races jumped to see the tracks.
   - (D) People who entered the races just showed up.

4. What is an antonym for *permanent*?
   - (A) curly
   - (B) fixed
   - (C) structured
   - (D) temporary

5. Why might Rowles, Livingstone, and Desbrow have wanted to make a lot of karts in a short amount of time?

____

____

____

____

____

____

____

____

____

© Shell Education

Name: ______________________________ Date: ________________

Directions: Closely read these texts. Write a dialogue the two authors might have had with each other related to go-kart safety.

Close-Reading Texts

Go-Kart Safety	A Race to Remember
Go-karting can be a lot of fun, but it can be dangerous, too. People should always make sure to wear helmets and safety glasses when they are riding go-karts. They should also check to be sure that their clothes and hair cannot catch on any of the moving parts. Before people get into go-karts, workers usually check to make sure that each go-kart is working properly. People should not ride any go-karts that are making weird noises or not running well.	After going over the safety rules, they each had a one-on-one lesson with an instructor. Hank's instructor taught him the importance of speed, while Timmy's instructor focused on patience and safety. "Slow and steady wins the race," Timmy's instructor kept saying.

Name: ______________________________ Date: ______________

Directions: Closely read these texts. Then, reread Go-Kart History. Compare the structures of each text by matching the structure to the text. Explain why you chose that structure for each title.

Close-Reading Texts

All About Go-Karts	In the Driver's Seat
Go-kart racing is sometimes called *karting*. People who participate in this sport learn how to drive go-karts, which look a lot like race cars. They race around a track, competing with one another to see who can be the fastest driver, similar to other auto races. Some amusement parks have outdoor go-kart racing tracks. And some companies have created indoor go-kart racing tracks in large buildings.	There are three kinds of go-kart races, and the first type is sprint races. These are very short races. Usually, the track for a sprint race forms an oval that is between 0.25–1 miles (0.4–1.6 kilometers) long. Most of these sprint races last about 15 minutes or less. The most important thing that a person needs to win a sprint race is speed. The faster their go-kart can safely go, the more likely they are to win.

Text Structures

chronology compare-contrast problem-solution

Text	Text Structure	How You Know
All About Go-Karts		
In the Driver's Seat		
Go-Kart History		

© Shell Education

Name: ______________________________ Date: ______________

Directions: Think about the texts from this unit. Then, respond to the prompt.

You are an announcer in "A Race to Remember." This means that you explain the action on the track to the audience as it happens. Write what you would have announced during the race.

© Shell Education

Name: ______________________ Date: ____________

Directions: Reread the fiction texts from week 2 and study the time line on page 221. Make a time line to detail key events from the story from beginning to end.

1	
2	
3	
4	
5	
6	
7	

 © Shell Education

Standards Correlations

Shell Education is committed to producing educational materials that are research and standards based. To support this effort, this resource is correlated to the academic standards of all 50 states, the District of Columbia, the Department of Defense Dependent Schools, and the Canadian provinces. A correlation is also provided for key professional educational organizations.

To print a customized correlation report for your state, visit our website at **www.tcmpub.com/administrators/correlations** and follow the online directions. If you require assistance in printing correlation reports, please contact the Customer Service Department at 1-800-858-7339.

Standards Overview

The Every Student Succeeds Act (ESSA) mandates that all states adopt challenging academic standards that help students meet the goal of college and career readiness. While many states already adopted academic standards prior to ESSA, the act continues to hold states accountable for detailed and comprehensive standards. Standardware is also used to develop standardized tests to evaluate students' academic progress. State standards are used in the development of our resources, so educators can be assured they meet state academic requirements.

College and Career Readiness

Today's college and career readiness (CCR) standards offer guidelines for preparing K–12 students with the knowledge and skills that are necessary to succeed in postsecondary job training and education. CCR standards include the Common Core State Standards as well as other state-adopted standards such as the Texas Essential Knowledge and Skills. The standards found on page 228 describe the content presented throughout the lessons.

TESOL and WIDA Standards

English language development standards are integrated within each lesson to enable English learners to work toward proficiency in English while learning content–developing the skills and confidence in listening, speaking, reading, and writing. The standards found in the digital resources describe the language objectives presented throughout the lessons

Standards Correlations *(cont.)*

180 Days of Reading for Fifth Grade, 2nd Edition, offers a full page of daily reading comprehension and word analysis practice activities for each day of the school year.

Every fifth grade unit provides questions and activities tied to a wide variety of language arts standards, providing students opportunities for regular practice in reading comprehension, word recognition, and writing. The focus of the first two weeks in each unit alternates between nonfiction and fiction standards, with the third week focusing on both, as students read nontraditional texts and complete paired-text activities.

Reading Comprehension
Read and comprehend complex literary and informational texts independently and proficiently.
Read closely to determine what the text says explicitly. Ask and answer questions about the text and make logical inferences.
Determine central ideas or themes of a text and analyze their development; summarize the key supporting details and ideas.
Analyze how and why individuals, events, or ideas develop and interact over the course of a text.
Recognize and analyze genre-specific characteristics, structures, and purposes within and across diverse texts.
Use metacognitive skills to both develop and deepen comprehension of texts.
Analyze how two or more texts address similar themes or topics to build knowledge or to compare the approaches the authors take.
Assess how point of view or purpose shapes the content and style of texts.
Reading Foundational Skills
Know and apply grade-level phonics and word analysis skills in decoding words.
Language and Vocabulary Acquisition
Determine or clarify the meaning of unknown and multiple-meaning words and phrases by using context clues, analyzing meaningful word parts, and consulting general and specialized reference materials, as appropriate.
Demonstrate understanding of figurative language, word relationships, and nuances in word meanings.
Writing
Produce clear and coherent writing in which the development, organization, and style are appropriate to task, purpose, genre, and audience.
Respond to and draw evidence from literary or informational texts to show analysis, reflection, and research.

© Shell Education

Writing Rubric

Score students' written responses using this rubric. Display the rubric for students to reference as they write. A student version of this rubric is provided in the digital resources.

Points	Criteria
4	• Uses an appropriate organizational sequence to produce very clear and coherent writing. • Uses descriptive language that develops or clarifies ideas. • Engages the reader. • Uses a style very appropriate to task, purpose, and audience.
3	• Uses an organizational sequence to produce clear and coherent writing. • Uses descriptive language that develops or clarifies ideas. • Engages the reader. • Uses a style appropriate to task, purpose, and audience.
2	• Uses an organizational sequence to produce somewhat clear and coherent writing. • Uses some descriptive language that develops or clarifies ideas. • Engages the reader in some way. • Uses a style somewhat appropriate to task, purpose, and audience.
1	• Does not use an organized sequence; the writing is not clear or coherent. • Uses little descriptive language to develop or clarify ideas. • Does not engage the reader. • Does not use a style appropriate to task, purpose, or audience.
0	• Offers no writing or does not respond to the assignment presented.

References Cited

Gough, Philip B., and William E. Tunmer. 1986. "Decoding, Reading, and Reading Disability." *Remedial and Special Education* 7 (1): 6–10.

Marzano, Robert. 2010. "When Practice Makes Perfect...Sense." *Educational Leadership* 68 (3): 81–83.

National Reading Panel. 2000. *Report of the National Reading Panel: Teaching Children to Read. Report of the Subgroups*. Washington, D.C.: U.S. Department of Health and Human Services, National Institutes of Health.

Scarborough, Hollis S. 2001. "Connecting Early Language and Literacy to Later Reading (Dis)abilities: Evidence, Theory, and Practice." In *Handbook of Early Literacy Research*, edited by Susan B. Neuman and David K. Dickinson, 97–110. New York: Guilford.

Soalt, Jennifer. 2005. "Bringing Together Fictional and Informational Texts to Improve Comprehension." *The Reading Teacher* 58 (7): 680–683.

Answer Key

Unit 1

Week 1

Day 1 (page 11)

1. B
2. D
3. A
4. D

Day 2 (page 12)

1. A
2. D
3. B
4. B

Day 3 (page 13)

1. D
2. C
3. Cereal that has whole grains and low sugar is good for you.
4. Sample response: The author would say my favorite cereal is not healthy because it has a lot of sugar.

Day 4 (page 15)

1. A
2. C
3. D
4. A
5. Sample responses:
   Event 2: Kellogg worked then managed a sanitarium.
   Event 3: Kellogg wanted the people in the sanitarium to eat healthier food.
   Event 4: Kellogg discovered breakfast flakes by accident.
   Event 5: Kellogg grew his discovery into a successful business.

Day 5 (page 16)

Responses should explain the best breakfast options that anyone can make using details and evidence from the one or more texts to support their ideas.

Week 2

Day 1 (page 17)

1. C
2. B
3. A
4. B

Day 2 (page 18)

1. C
2. B
3. A
4. D

Day 3 (page 19)

1. D
2. A
3. Henry also won a tour of the local cereal factory, a year's worth of cereal, and a chance to create his own cereal.
4. Sample response: I would hope to win the newest cell phone, a year's plan with unlimited data, and free games.

Day 4 (page 21)

1. B
2. A
3. D
4. D
5. Sample responses:
   Events: Henry selected the base and added ingredients. Henry watched as the machines put his cereal together. Henry and his family went home to try out his cereal.
   Resolution: Everyone enjoyed Henry's cereal, except his parents avoided the gummy worms.

Day 5 (page 22)

Stories should be about times they made something unusual for breakfast, using a variety of transitional words, phrases, and clauses to manage the sequence of events.

Week 3

Day 1 (page 24)

1. A
2. A
3. C
4. B
5. Sample response: I would not like to try Henry's cereal because I don't think gummy worms go well with milk, and I am not a fan of marshmallows.

Day 2 (page 25)

Sample response: Scrambled eggs will give Henry protein. A glass of orange juice will give him fruit. Some oatmeal will give him grains.

Day 3 (page 26)

Sample responses:

Ingredients in Healthy Cereals: whole grains, nuts, fruits

Ingredients in Unhealthy Cereals: sugar, marshmallows, candy, chocolate chips

Henry's cereal was not very healthy. It had three ingredients that have a lot of sugar.

Day 4 (page 27)

Stories should tell about times in which they motivate friends to eat healthy breakfasts that they create together.

Day 5 (page 28)

Cereal box covers should include the names of original cereals and descriptions of the ingredients.

Unit 2

Week 1

Day 1 (page 29)

1. D
2. C
3. B
4. D

Day 2 (page 30)

1. A
2. A
3. B
4. C

Day 3 (page 31)

1. B
2. B
3. Examples include a variation of the following: Surface currents bring warm water from the equator toward the poles. It cools and sinks. Deeper currents start at the poles. The deep water flows away from the poles into the ocean basins. Deep water rises to the surface, and the currents continue.
4. Sample response: The ocean helps keep Earth from warming up. Strong currents and waves can damage ships and people on land.

© Shell Education

Answer Key *(cont.)*

Day 4 (page 33)

1. C
2. C
3. A
4. B
5.

Effects
An algal bloom occurs.
The plants and algae below produce less oxygen.
Animals in the water and people who drink the water can get sick.

Day 5 (page 34)

Answers should explain how oceans are important to Earth.

Week 2

Day 1 (page 35)

1. B
2. D
3. C
4. D

Day 2 (page 36)

1. C
2. B
3. A
4. D

Day 3 (page 37)

1. B
2. A
3. The corals used to be beautiful and full of color and life.
4. Sample response: Steve will find out that something is causing the changes to the coral reef.

Day 4 (page 39)

1. A
2. C
3. A
4. B
5. **Research Goal:** He wanted to test the idea if oxygen levels and temperature affected the health of corals.
   Experimental Plan: He measure temperatures, amount of bubbles, and oxygen levels around the reef.
   Results: Higher temperatures had fewer healthy coral. Fewer organisms were in places with higher temperatures.
   Sharing Data: He submitted a paper to NABS.

Day 5 (page 40)

Answers should include written stories about ocean creatures who discover unusual things, using descriptive details and developing a clear sequence of events.

Week 3

Day 1 (page 42)

1. D
2. C
3. D
4. D
5. Sample response: I think the author is more excited than nervous. They describe all the events with a lot of excitement, and they reassure themselves that everything will be okay.

Day 2 (page 43)

Ocean Life: Plankton: Phytoplankton need sunlight to grow; Phytoplankton need nutrients to create an algal bloom.
World Traveler: Plankton live in the ocean; Dead zones have little oxygen.
Phytoplankton Journal: Algal blooms can be seen from space.

Day 3 (page 44)

Steve: excited; He said he was excited to learn more.

Tom: pleased; He said this would be great for science.

Phytoplankton: excited; Exciting things are happening.

Day 4 (page 45)

Answers should explain why students agree or disagree that people should be mindful of ocean pollution.

Day 5 (page 46)

Answers should describe what happens during an algal bloom using descriptive words and sensory details to explain the events.

Unit 3

Week 1

Day 1 (page 47)

1. D
2. A
3. B
4. D

Day 2 (page 48)

1. D
2. B
3. C
4. D

Day 3 (page 49)

1. C
2. C
3. Malls have to offer things that people cannot find online.
4. Sample response: Malls have improved because there is a lot more to do there than just shop.

Day 4 (page 51)

1. B
2. B
3. A
4. A
5. Sample responses:
   Mall of America: St. Paul, MN; flight simulator; mirror maze; mini-golf; theme park; over 520 stores
   Dubai Mall: United Arab Emirates; over 1,000 stores; skating rink; hotel
   Both: very large, movie theater; aquarium; more than a day to visit the whole mall

Day 5 (page 52)

Answers should include detailed plans for a day at the Mall of America or the Dubai Mall using facts and details from the text.

Week 2

Day 1 (page 53)

1. B
2. A
3. B
4. C

Day 2 (page 54)

1. A
2. A
3. D
4. B

Answer Key (cont.)

Day 3 (page 55)

1. B
2. A
3. She thought the craziness would end.
4. Sample response: They were nervous about what had happened.

Day 4 (page 57)

1. D
2. A
3. C
4. A
5. Sample responses:
   clever: using the QR code to find clues to return home
   adventurous: visiting malls around the world
   hopeful: selecting the mall they came from

Day 5 (page 58)

Stories should tell about times students found something strange at a mall.

Week 3

Day 1 (page 60)

1. A
2. A
3. B
4. D
5. Sample response: I would like to visit the Morocco Mall so that I could see the fish by riding the elevator.

Day 2 (page 61)

Sample responses:

1. Malls have restaurants. Malls have rollercoasters. Malls have aquariums.
2. People who like food can eat at different kinds of restaurants. People who like rides can go to the theme park in the mall. People who like movies can see new flicks.

Day 3 (page 62)

Sample responses:

Before Malls Were Built	After Malls Were Build
People shopped in downtown areas. People who did not live close to town had to travel far to shop.	There are different kinds of stores and shops all in one location. Malls are close to where people live, so they do not need to travel far to shop.
Both	
People shop in person. People go to where the shops are.	

Day 4 (page 63)

Responses should be letters written to convince students' families that they should take trips to certain malls from the texts.

Day 5 (page 64)

Responses should be completed fact sheets about malls students researched.

Unit 4

Week 1

Day 1 (page 65)

1. A
2. D
3. C
4. B

Day 2 (page 66)

1. B
2. A
3. D
4. A

Day 3 (page 67)

1. B
2. A
3. pizza pan, paddle, oven
4. Sample response: I like plain cheese pizza. I would never eat anchovies on pizza.

Day 4 (page 69)

1. B
2. C
3. B
4. D
5. **Japan:** seafood, pancake dough
   India: naan, pepperoni, tandoori chicken, tofu, chili flakes, ketchup
   Australia: pepperoni, lamb, eggs, ham, pineapple, pumpkin, shrimp

Day 5 (page 70)

Responses should describe which pizzas from the text students would be most interested in eating and support their ideas with reasons, facts, and details.

Week 2

Day 1 (page 71)

1. D
2. B
3. C
4. C

Day 2 (page 72)

1. D
2. A
3. D
4. A

Day 3 (page 73)

1. C
2. B
3. His dad encouraged him. His mom made a banner.
4. Sample response: Kevin is determined. He sets a goal and pushes through to achieve it.

Day 4 (page 75)

1. B
2. A
3. A
4. D
5. Sample response: He eventually made it through the entire recipe list. Kevin decided to go with a simple but effective recipe. The judges praised him for taking a simple recipe and making it unique.

© Shell Education

Answer Key *(cont.)*

Day 5 (page 76)

Responses should explain criteria students would be looking for as a judge at the cook off to determine the winning dish, and then describe a favorite food of their own that meets these criteria.

Week 3

Day 1 (page 78)

1. B
2. B
3. C
4. C
5. Sample response: The author described the restaurant as the tastiest place in town. The author described the stone oven pizza as the star of the show. They also said that each pizza was delightful, and that it made for an incredible pizza experience.

Day 2 (page 79)

Sample response: BBQ Chicken Delight; Crust: flour, yeast, water, red pepper flakes; Sauce: BBQ sauce; Toppings: grilled chicken, mozzarella cheese, red pepper slices

Day 3 (page 80)

Chefs: Dough: flour, yeast, water; Sauce: tomato sauce; Toppings: toppings and cheese

Kevin: Dough: thick and crisp; Sauce: fresh sauce from ripened garden tomatoes; Toppings: mozzarella, toppings

Day 4 (page 81)

Stories should be about having a challenging experience making pizza.

Day 5 (page 82)

Responses should be reviews of favorite restaurant foods or favorite meals.

Unit 5

Week 1

Day 1 (page 83)

1. B
2. D
3. A
4. B

Day 2 (page 84)

1. D
2. A
3. A
4. D

Day 3 (page 85)

1. D
2. C
3. They have found ways to stay cool and get enough water.
4. Sample response: I would like to visit the Kalahari Desert. There are plants and animals there that I don't get to see every day.

Day 4 (page 87)

1. C
2. B
3. C
4. B
5. Sample response: Their eyes have dark circles that act like sunglasses. They have special patches of skin on their bellies that absorb the sunlight. They have sharp claws that are used for digging burrows and looking for food.

Day 5 (page 88)

Responses should each describe a day in the life of a meerkat.

Week 2

Day 1 (page 89)

1. B
2. A
3. C
4. C

Day 2 (page 90)

1. B
2. C
3. A
4. D

Day 3 (page 91)

1. C
2. C
3. snakes, large animals, other unknown predators
4. Sample response: Yes, Miles will stick by Mort because the tall grass can be dangerous, and Mort saved his life once before.

Day 4 (page 93)

1. B
2. A
3. A
4. D
5.

Effect
They had escape holes ready in case of danger.
The snake chased after him.
The snake slithered away.

Day 5 (page 94)

Answers should include a rewritten story from the point of view of the snake, using a variety of transitional words, phrases, and clauses to manage the sequence of events.

Week 3

Day 1 (page 96)

1. C
2. D
3. D
4. C
5. Responses should explain what students' find most interesting about meerkats.

Day 2 (page 97)

Physical Traits: dark circles around their eyes act like sunglasses; skin patches on bellies absorb sunlight; pointed snouts; sharp claws

Behavioral: live in underground tunnels; mobs work together to hunt, watch for predators, and raise young; sleep in piles; stand upright; elders teach their young; the young choose an elder

Day 3 (page 98)

Lion: hunts for small animals; black mane

Gemsbok: can live long without water; get water from plants

Meerkat: small and furry; sharp claws; long tails; stand upright

What They Have In Common: live in the desert

Day 4 (page 99)

Responses should have plans for a series of documentary videos with descriptive facts about meerkats.

Answer Key *(cont.)*

Day 5 (page 100)

Responses should be zoo panels for animals that lives in the Kalahari Desert.

Unit 6

Week 1

Day 1 (page 101)

1. B
2. C
3. B
4. D

Day 2 (page 102)

1. A
2. B
3. C
4. C

Day 3 (page 103)

1. B
2. D
3. Objects that have too much mass can eventually form black holes. The gravity is so great that not even light can escape.
4. Sample response: I think scientists will discover more black holes in the Milky Way because they are always finding new objects in space.

Day 4 (page 105)

1. C
2. C
3. B
4. D
5.

Hubble	James Webb
fourth space telescope to be put into space; looked at objects in outer space through the visible spectrum; cannot see through space dust	launched on December 25, 2021; mirror is almost three times wider; can see objects that are fainter and further away; sees the light that is in the infrared; can see stuff behind huge clouds of space dust
Both	
led to a lot of discoveries; space telescopes	

Day 5 (page 106)

Responses should explain what lies in space beyond Earth, developing the topic with facts, definitions, concrete details, quotations from one or more texts, or other information and examples.

Week 2

Day 1 (page 107)

1. D
2. B
3. A
4. A

Day 2 (page 108)

1. B
2. A
3. B
4. C

Day 3 (page 109)

1. D
2. D
3. Naomi was ready to write down more facts about space from a short video.
4. Sample response: I would want to try being in zero gravity if I went to space camp.

Day 4 (page 111)

1. B
2. C
3. D
4. A
5. **Europa:** icy surface; one of Jupiter's moons
   Jupiter: giant spinning ball of gas with empty space around it; held in orbit by the sun's gravity
   earthquake: shaking; cracking ice below her
   gravity: feet came off the ground; floating

Day 5 (page 112)

Responses should include written stories about a day students went to space, orienting the reader by establishing a situation and introducing a narrator and/or characters, and organizing an event sequence that unfolds naturally.

Week 3

Day 1 (page 114)

1. D
2. B
3. B
4. A
5. Answers should describe what students think Naomi and her crew will do on their way to Europa and once they arrive there.

Day 2 (page 115)

Text	Interjection	Purpose or Meaning
Let's Talk Science	Ooh!	to show the classmates thought going to space camp was interesting
A Strange Trip to Europa	Whew!	to show that Naomi is relieved it was a dream
Naomi's Adventure Comic	Whoa!	to show Naomi is shocked by what she is seeing

Day 3 (page 116)

Star Stuff: anxious; She is starting a new school year and did not sleep well.

Let's Talk Science: relieved; She learned other students liked space and that they would be learning about space.

Naomi's Comic Adventure: excited; She notices how beautiful it is and says she has been dreaming of this day.

Day 4 (page 117)

Responses should explain why students would or would not want to be astronauts when they grow up, linking their opinions and reasons using words, phrases, and clauses.

 © Shell Education

Answer Key *(cont.)*

Day 5 (page 118)

Comics should include flights with Galactic Travel Tours, describing where they go and what they see and do, and using speech bubbles to show dialogue.

Unit 7

Week 1

Day 1 (page 119)

1. C
2. B
3. A
4. C

Day 2 (page 120)

1. C
2. A
3. A
4. C

Day 3 (page 121)

1. D
2. B
3. When exactly the Māori came to New Zealand is still uncertain.
4. Answers should describe images students would use to support the text.

Day 4 (page 123)

1. D
2. D
3. C
4. A
5. **South Island:** mountains for skiing; miles of beaches, forests, and lakes

   North Island: has the capital of Willington and the largest city, Auckland; volcanoes, hot springs, warmer

   Animals: fish, whales, dolphins, birds, kiwis

   Sports: rugby, cricket

Day 5 (page 124)

Responses should explain how life in New Zealand compares to where students live, using information and examples from one or more texts to support their ideas.

Week 2

Day 1 (page 125)

1. A
2. D
3. B
4. A

Day 2 (page 126)

1. A
2. D
3. C
4. D

Day 3 (page 127)

1. B
2. C
3. the whale rider
4. Sample response: They can give details about their history to explain events and customs.

Day 4 (page 129)

1. B
2. C
3. C
4. D
5. Sample responses:

1. Koa welcomes everyone to the festival.
2. Kai and Jacob fill their plates at the buffet.
3. Jacob meets Manu, and Manu asks questions about Canada.
4. Jacob learns more about Māori culture from Kaia and Manu.

Day 5 (page 130)

Written letters should be addressed to imaginary pen pals, describing what students' lives are like.

Week 3

Day 1 (page 132)

1. C
2. D
3. C
4. B
5. Answers should include a form of traditional or cultural artwork students know of or have seen, such as American Indian pottery.

Day 2 (page 133)

Sample responses:

"The Māori" Summary: People aren't really sure when the Māori came to New Zealand, but they are Polynesian and skilled sailors.

"Blog Post from Kaia" Summary: The Māori have many kinds of performances to share different parts of their culture. One part is strength and pride of the tribe. Another represents parts of nature and passion.

Day 3 (page 134)

Sample responses:

Preparing for the Festival: fictional story, mentions Māori, creates a setting for the story

Both: talk about Auckland, New Zealand

Auckland, New Zealand: informational text, gives details about things to do and see in Auckland

Day 4 (page 135)

Responses should explain what students find to be the most interesting aspects of the Māori culture and provide logically ordered reasons that are supported by facts and details.

Day 5 (page 136)

Responses should be blog posts about families or other cultural traditions.

Unit 8

Week 1

Day 1 (page 137)

1. C
2. D
3. A
4. C

Day 2 (page 138)

1. B
2. D
3. C
4. C

Day 3 (page 139)

1. D
2. C
3. If rowers do not work as a team, the boat will not move smoothly.
4. Sample response: Rowers work as a team. Water skiers can work alone or as a team, and they have skis instead of a boat.

Answer Key *(cont.)*

Day 4 (page 141)

1. C
2. C
3. D
4. A
5. Sample responses:
   Event 2: After many years, the Greeks stopped having the Games.
   Event 3: For a long time, there were no Games.
   Event 4: In 1896, the modern Olympics were held in Athens.

Day 5 (page 142)

Written stories should be from the views of spectators at either the ancient or modern Olympics and include descriptive details.

Week 2

Day 1 (page 143)

1. C
2. A
3. B
4. A

Day 2 (page 144)

1. D
2. B
3. B
4. C

Day 3 (page 145)

1. A
2. B
3. Sammy was nervous about not being a good swimmer. She was excited about learning to swim better.
4. Sample response: I wish I was better at basketball. I am tall, and people think I should play basketball, but I am not good at it.

Day 4 (page 147)

1. C
2. C
3. B
4. A
5. Sample responses:
   1. Lie down on your left side.
   2. Extend your left arm above your head, palm facing down. Rest your head on the upper part of your arm.
   3. Place your right hand across your chest and onto the floor in front of you.
   4. Bend your knees at a 90-degree angle.
   5. Pull your knees toward your chest and kick in the opposite direction.
   6. Straighten both legs and bring them back to the starting position.

Day 5 (page 148)

Responses should include written steps to something students can teach others to do, linking ideas using words, phrases, and clauses.

Week 3

Day 1 (page 150)

1. A
2. C
3. D
4. C
5. Sample response: I want to learn to paint and enter a painting in the fair. I can watch videos of painters and try to do what they do on their canvases.

Day 2 (page 151)

Great Form!: Third person; Sammy is not telling the story herself; Sammy is excited about the idea of going to the Olympics when she first starts swimming lessons.

An Interview with Sammy: First person; Sammy is explaining things herself; Sammy explains that she did not consider the Olympics until long after she started swimming lessons.

Day 3 (page 152)

Fencing: The object is to touch your opponent with your sword; it is an individual sport; lots of moves to learn.

Rowing: uses a boat and oars; it is a team sport; rowers must work together.

Both: take a lot of practice

Day 4 (page 153)

Responses should include diary entries written as if students were Sammy having just completed her first swimming lesson. Answers should also include a picture.

Day 5 (page 154)

Responses should include interviews between students and famous athletes, writing the interviews as scripts.

Unit 9

Week 1

Day 1 (page 155)

1. B
2. B
3. A
4. D

Day 2 (page 156)

1. A
2. C
3. D
4. D

Day 3 (page 157)

1. B
2. C
3. when disasters strike
4. Sample response: We may have a flood and not be able to live in our house.

Day 4 (page 159)

1. B
2. C
3. D
4. D
5. She gave these things to the soldiers; She became ill; She went to Europe and learned about the Red Cross.

 © Shell Education

Answer Key *(cont.)*

Day 5 (page 160)

Responses should explain how nursing has changed over the years, using information and examples from both texts to support ideas.

Week 2

Day 1 (page 161)

1. B
2. A
3. C
4. B

Day 2 (page 162)

1. D
2. C
3. A
4. A

Day 3 (page 163)

1. C
2. B
3. Kenyon's family didn't know where to go, and they were running low on gas.
4. Sample response: It's important to be prepared ahead of time so that you know what you will do and where you will go during a natural disaster.

Day 4 (page 165)

1. B
2. D
3. C
4. B
5. **Emily:** earthquake; hid under a table
Zahara: tornado; received support from the Red Cross
Kenyon: wildfire; sought shelter with the Red Cross
Response to Camp: excited about learning survival skills and participating in fun activities

Day 5 (page 166)

Written stories should be about attending camps where students meet new people.

Week 3

Day 1 (page 168)

1. C
2. D
3. A
4. C
5. Sample response: I might pack a blanket, my phone, my solar phone charger, and my favorite stuffed animal.

Day 2 (page 169)

Responses should include words closely related to natural disasters, such as: earthquakes, emergency kits, evacuation plans, floods, and tornadoes.

Day 3 (page 170)

The Red Cross: volunteers treat people who need healthcare; rescue dogs will sometimes help

Zaharah and the Tornado: brought first aid with them; helped fix and rebuild the homes

Both: volunteers bring food and water; provide shelter

Day 4 (page 171)

Answers should include thank you letters to nurses or Red Cross volunteers for the work they do.

Day 5 (page 172)

Answers should include infographics for nursing or the Red Cross using information from the texts.

Unit 10

Week 1

Day 1 (page 173)

1. A
2. B
3. C
4. C

Day 2 (page 174)

1. B
2. B
3. A
4. C

Day 3 (page 175)

1. B
2. C
3. Jeet Kune Do and Chun Kuk Do
4. Sample response: The actors used martial arts in movies, and that's how they became famous.

Day 4 (page 177)

1. C
2. A
3. A
4. C
5. **China:** began as a way to hunt for food and train soldiers; earliest is from the 5th century BCE; documents show hand-to-hand combat; called kung fu
Japan: started with samurai; used weapons; jujitsu does not use weapons; two types
Both: used for fighting wars

Day 5 (page 178)

Responses should compare and contrast two forms of martial arts using facts and details from both "Types of Martial Arts" and "A Brief History of Martial Arts."

Week 2

Day 1 (page 179)

1. D
2. D
3. B
4. C

Day 2 (page 180)

1. C
2. B
3. D
4. A

Day 3 (page 181)

1. B
2. D
3. Matt thought he would learn to kick and fight, but he learned that karate is more about the mind and body working together.
4. Sample response: I don't like to give up on things, so I would stick with it. I may come to like it after all.

Day 4 (page 183)

1. C
2. A
3. C
4. D
5. Sample responses:
   2. Matt filled out an application to take his first karate test.
   3. Matt was tested on the movements, and he took a written test.
   4. Matt passed his test and was glad he stuck with it.

Answer Key (cont.)

Day 5 (page 184)

Stories should be about taking karate lessons with friends.

Week 3

Day 1 (page 186)

1. C
2. B
3. D
4. A
5. Sample response: The ad definitely motivates me to sign up for martial arts classes. I have a lot of different types to choose from, and the kids sound really excited to be there.

Day 2 (page 187)

Sample response: I would like to try jujitsu. It has an interesting history, and it offers me a way to improve and defend myself. Check students illustrations.

Day 3 (page 188)

Matt: wanted to be like the martial arts actors

Samurai: important military nobility; used weapons; they started martial arts in Japan

Both: practice martial arts

Day 4 (page 189)

Responses should explain the meaning of martial arts being "about mind and body working together," and describe how it is used in another activity using precise language and vocabulary to develop their ideas.

Day 5 (page 190)

Responses should include written radio ads to persuade others to sign up for a sport students play, using dialogue similar to the radio ad and should include a persuasive technique such as repetition, a celebrity endorsement, or an appeal to others' emotions.

Unit 11

Week 1

Day 1 (page 191)

1. A
2. D
3. A
4. C

Day 2 (page 192)

1. A
2. D
3. D
4. C

Day 3 (page 193)

1. D
2. C
3. The brain replaces chemicals it needs, heals, and builds up the body's immune system and muscles.
4. Sample response: I agree. When I sleep well, I think clearly in school and I am not cranky like when I do not sleep well.

Day 4 (page 195)

1. D
2. D
3. B
4. C
5. Sample response: Keep your body in a routine by going to bed at the same time every night; Do something calming right before bedtime, such as taking a warm bath or reading; Limit sodas, iced tea, and other foods and drinks that contain caffeine.

Day 5 (page 196)

Letters to friends should explain why they should get more sleep, and how to sleep better, supporting reasons with facts and details from at least one text.

Week 2

Day 1 (page 197)

1. D
2. B
3. D
4. A

Day 2 (page 198)

1. A
2. B
3. D
4. A

Day 3 (page 199)

1. A
2. D
3. Hallie is stressed about getting Isaac to feel better, but she's hopeful because she has tips from the vet.
4. Sample response: A hiding place could make Isaac feel safe and cozy, which might make him less stressed.

Day 4 (page 201)

1. D
2. B
3. A
4. D
5. Sample responses:
    1. Isaac tried some new food.
    2. Hallie and Isaac played with his toy mice and explored the house.
    3. Hallie made Isaac a scratch post.
    4. Isaac napped in his new hiding place.

Day 5 (page 202)

Responses should describe dreams students have had recently and explain how they made them feel when they woke up.

Week 3

Day 1 (page 204)

1. D
2. C
3. A
4. C
5. Sample response: When I have trouble sleeping, I heat up and drink a glass of milk and add a little honey. I usually fall right to sleep after I drink it.

Day 2 (page 205)

Sample responses:

1. Your body does a lot while you sleep.
2. Your brain stays busy while you sleep.
3. Special equipment can monitor your sleep.
4. Stress can cause cats to have trouble sleeping.

© Shell Education

Answer Key *(cont.)*

Day 3 (page 206)

Sweet Dreams: problem-solution; You can do a lot to help you fall asleep, like following a routine and exercising during the day.

Isaac the House Cat: problem-solution; Isaac's tries different things to sleep better.

Day 4 (page 207)

Responses should include details from sleep diaries for several nights.

Day 5 (page 208)

Poems should be about sleeping and include rhyme patterns and illustrations.

Unit 12

Week 1

Day 1 (page 209)

1. C
2. A
3. B
4. B

Day 2 (page 210)

1. B
2. A
3. D
4. A

Day 3 (page 211)

1. C
2. B
3. Sample response: This helps children stay safe when driving go-karts.
4. Sample response: I think it is kind of hard because there are a lot of parts to a go-kart.

Day 4 (page 213)

1. C
2. D
3. B
4. D
5. **Sprint Races:** short; between one quarter mile and one mile long; about 15 minutes long; require speed
   Endurance Races: 30 to 45 minutes long; need a kart that will last and can go the same speed for the whole race
   Both: types of go-kart races; you can do any kind of race; exciting and popular

Day 5 (page 214)

Responses should explain why go-karting is or is not a good sport to participate in, with logically ordered reasons supported by facts and details.

Week 2

Day 1 (page 215)

1. D
2. C
3. C
4. C

Day 2 (page 216)

1. B
2. D
3. C
4. C

Day 3 (page 217)

1. B
2. C
3. Timmy had to be extra careful, wear extra padding, and take go-karting classes.
4. Sample response: Timmy was probably really excited to start driving a go-kart.

Day 4 (page 219)

1. D
2. A
3. D
4. C
5. Sample responses:
   1. They take lessons with instructors.
   2. Timmy is discouraged, but he keeps trying.
   3. Hank causes a crash, and other drivers lose control.

Day 5 (page 220)

Stories should be about entering go-kart races, using dialogue, description, and pacing to effectively develop the story.

Week 3

Day 1 (page 222)

1. D
2. A
3. B
4. D
5. Sample response: They may have wanted to help go-karting become popular with a lot of people.

Day 2 (page 223)

Sample responses: It's important to be safe when go-karting. Be sure you don't go too fast. And, remember to wear a helmet and safety glasses. That will keep you safe in case something goes wrong.

Day 3 (page 224)

1. **All About Go-Karts:** problem-solution; Go-karts can be used in place of real cars to race.
2. **In the Driver's Seat:** compare and contrast; There are details about two of three different types of races.
3. **Go-Kart History:** chronology; Dates explain when events happened in order

Day 4 (page 225)

Race announcements should be written from the perspective of announcers in "A Race to Remember."

Day 5 (page 226)

Responses should show time lines detailing key events from the whole story of Hank and Timmy from beginning to end.

Digital Resources

Accessing the Digital Resources

The digital resources can be downloaded by following these steps:

1. Go to **www.tcmpub.com/digital**
2. Use the 13-digit ISBN number to redeem the digital resources.
3. Respond to the question using the book.
4. Follow the prompts on the Content Cloud website to sign in or create a new account.
5. The content redeemed will appear on your My Content screen. Click on the product to look through the digital resources. All file resources are available for download. Select files can be previewed, opened, and shared.

For questions and assistance with your ISBN redemption, please contact Shell Education.

email: customerservice@tcmpub.com

phone: 800-858-7339

Contents of the Digital Resources

- Standards Correlations
- Writing Rubric
- Fluency Rubric
- Class and Individual Analysis Sheets